MISTAKEN IDENTITY

MISTAKEN IDENTITY

A GUIDE TO LETTING GO
of a Past that's Holding You Back

DOUG DANE

Forefront
BOOKS

Mistaken Identity: A Guide to Letting Go of a Past that's Holding You Back

Published by Forefront Books.
Distributed by Simon & Schuster.

Library of Congress Control Number: 2022922665
Print ISBN: 978-1-63763-166-9
E-book ISBN: 978-1-63763-167-6
Cover Design by Bruce Gore, Gore Studio, Inc.
Interior Design by PerfecType, Nashville, TN

This book is dedicated to my daughter. You came into my life at just the right time, and I realized I was worth more than I felt I was. You inspired me to be a better man, a better father, and a better person to help the world.

CONTENTS

PROLOGUE

Dark Past, Bright Future

■ *The Toronto Star, April 6, 2002*

Before I was born, I was set up for abuse. Born in October 1963 to a woman who had already abandoned three children to the child welfare system, I was placed for adoption into an abusive environment. Ironically, I was placed by the Children's Aid Society, a sanctioned agency, mandated to protect children. The placement could not have been more wrong.

In a time when our national news is riddled with examples of childhood abuse, when we should have the resources to provide guaranteed safe havens for children, my story must be told. It is not good enough to shake our heads, pour out a small amount of disgust, then move on to brushing our teeth before we turn out the light and forget.

Stories like mine need to be placed before our consciousness until we as a society take responsibility. Complacent, aging bureaucracies and under-stimulated consciences must be revitalized before more lives are lost to physical or emotional death, crime, and the perpetuated cycle of abuse. The myth that we do all we can to protect children needs to be seen for what it is.

I am stepping forward with fear, anger and hope in the belief that my story can make a difference. I believe that others will relate to it, that a collective voice can make a difference, and that there are good people within a decaying, top-heavy system who will muster the courage to do what they know they should.

In my case, I have learned through interviews with the Children's Aid Society of the Waterloo Region and through files received through the Freedom of Information Act that grave errors were made. I was placed poorly and monitored dismally. Later, when police investigations and child welfare intervention were necessary, both failed me.

So, I pose the question: In the many situations of abuse that were part of my life, who was responsible? My adoptive parents? The child welfare system? The police? Or was it just me?

That last question, unfortunately, is what the child internalizes. Like other victims of childhood abuse, I took on the blame and the shame. Therein lies the crux of my story—that the damage done to children's psyches and souls, in a society as liberal and as enlightened as Canada's, is entirely preventable.

I was adopted as a six-month-old baby. The parents chosen for me were both alcoholics. Relatives knew. Friends knew. They had also been approved for a child eighteen months previously; he was adopted as a newborn. We became brothers.

From what I have gathered within the past year, it was the most rudimentary of home studies, yet it would have been simple to unearth that my parents were alcoholics and should never have been given the gift of one child, let alone two.

Instead, case notes indicate my father was "passive but quietly friendly and congenial" and that my mother "lacked the social graces of a very feminine woman." This man, whom the system turned into a father of two vulnerable boys, abused not only his own body but that of his equally abusive wife. This woman, whom the system turned into a mother, abused her body, her husband, and her two adopted sons.

Every day was a ritual of abuse and survival, permeated by the stink of stale beer and cigarettes amid the squalor of a living room turned into my mother's bedroom. My dad had to have a lock on his bedroom door because my mom, drunk and violent every day, would instigate fights with him.

The grind was the same: Get up, go to school, come home for lunch. We weren't allowed to stay in the safety of the school. No, filled with the dread of what might lay ahead, we had to return to our mother at home. Then it was back to school and home again for more.

Often, my brother and I would be assigned bizarre, crazy-making chores. On one occasion, my mother made me paint the living room to cover up the beer and bloodstains on the walls from her fights with my father. Other times, I would have to roll cigarettes for her while she ran around the house yelling and screaming.

Child welfare records bring that life back hauntingly for me. When I was six years old, notes were made by social workers because my mother had "suffered a nervous collapse." The child protection worker observed that "the home situation had deteriorated over the past few weeks. Mr. Dane had been drinking quite heavily and beating his wife. She had charged him with assault." There are notes that foster care was needed, that "the worker saw Mr. Dane as being burdened with troubles of the world" and that "Mrs. Dane had a previous mental breakdown two years earlier."

My brother and I were placed in a foster home on a farm for that summer and part of the fall. We liked the foster parents but missed our dog, Mitzi. Case notes indicate that there were six contacts during that time—two with our father, two with our mother, and two with both parents.

And then this: "Mrs. Dane returned home on Oct. 28, and the boys were returned. Mr. Dane had endeavored to remain away from his drinking, and Mrs. Dane had endeavored to maintain some stability in trying to work out the marriage. The boys were involved in the Scout program and hockey and Sunday school. Case was closed Jan. 28, 1971."

That was it, tidily worded and tucked away in the archives. Euphemisms work wonders! On paper.

In reality, as my brother and I advanced in age and collective misery, the daily rituals mutated into greater darkness.

After school, we'd wait (often outside the house because of Mom's drunkenness) for Dad to get home from work. My brother and I would stay out long enough for Mom to pass out drunk so that we'd be able to get in the house safely.

On worse nights or on weekends, we'd sit in Dad's locked room for safety from Mom when she came yelling and pounding on the door. If she did get ahold of Dad, the fights would be bloody.

Police visits became the norm for our neighborhood. Shame became my most constant companion.

> **Two boys abandoned by the agency that had found a mother figure for them.**

At least once a week, I ran away, coming back after midnight when I knew she would be passed out. At times, I stayed overnight at a safe home of our neighbors. Our neighbors were our guardian angels.

When I was twelve, the Children's Aid Society was once again called in to assist—this time by my mother. Again, they did nothing substantial to intervene and protect my brother and me.

Case notes state that she wanted information on counseling and that she "sounded very agitated, possibly inebriated. The children are finding the situation quite upsetting."

That's all. Two boys abandoned by the agency that had found a mother figure for them. Tokenism. A brief note to file. Case closed.

Finally one day, I was old enough and strong enough. When I came home from school, my dad was in the basement, and my mom was starting to beat on him. I put her in a headlock, carried her upstairs, and threw her out the side door. Locking her out, I called the police.

As they were putting her in the cruiser, she yelled to the police and the neighbors, "My son tried to murder me." I was thirteen years old.

There was a final note on this from the child welfare agency: "Mrs. Dane's alcoholism is getting worse, and she left the home on July 8. Mr. Dane met with a worker and seemed to be looking for a way to keep her out of the home now that she had left. Mr. Dane [was] advised to seek legal counsel."

Period. Case closed again.

With my mother gone, I could run the streets. Now a broken, sober man, my father suffered from the effects of alcoholism, bad memories of his World War

II experiences, and feelings of failure as a man and a father. And so it was that I fell into the clutches of a ring of sexual predators.

Four Kitchener-Waterloo men corralled twenty-three boys and persuaded us that our relationship was love. That's how desperate we were. That's how perverted they were. Two years of abuse culminated in my kidnapping when they took me to Halifax. I was fifteen.

I found my way home a week later. Soon afterwards, the police—two giants in uniform—presented me with what they knew and conducted a brief interview to gather more facts. Then they were gone. They didn't talk to my father or brother. They left me alone to carry the burden of shame.

In the copies of police reports I obtained, entire sections were whited out to protect the privacy of others involved. All I could see were a few typed notes of the interview with me, vague "footprints" left by the Children's Aid Society, the photographs that were seized, and the name of the stereo store and the Boy Scout troop the predators were involved with. (The four men were convicted on various sex charges in 1980 and received short sentences.)

More secrets, more shame!

I quit high school three times. In my heart, I knew I should stay in school, but I couldn't do it. Despite my high marks, I followed the path that had been laid out for me by the people who had abused me and by the authorities and professionals who had failed me.

> ## I could run the streets . . . I fell into the clutches of a ring of sexual predators.

The next fifteen years were the toughest. I tried almost every drug possible and broke free only because the altered state inflamed my feelings of inadequacy and shame. I was fortunate enough to experience the pain and paranoia caused by doing drugs and, thus, saved from disappearing into the sinkhole that childhood trauma often leads to. Searching for validation through success, I worked at a number of jobs, failed at businesses, went bankrupt, and eventually landed on my feet. I married twice and divorced twice. The feelings of being unaccepted and unsure of myself ate away at me. Little, dark, nasty, blathering voices always danced at the back of my consciousness.

Both my parents are gone now. I have survived the loss of a mother four times: my birth mother's abandonment, the eviction of my adoptive mother, my adoptive mother's death from cancer two years ago, and my birth mother's unwillingness to acknowledge me as her own now.

In therapy, I have worked on dealing with my losses and the aftershock of childhood abuse. Some people who have made a difference in my life—neighbors who cared, one cop who wanted to protect abused kids, a few teachers who made an impact, and two wives and

their families who were good people—were like delicate lilies along that path to healing.

Now I am successful in business and financially
secure. I have found four natural siblings and my birth
mother. And I am at long last beginning to see purpose in my life and to live in peace. Someone somewhere once astutely said, "The average person tiptoes
through life, hoping to make it safely to death." Something inside me—soul, self, truth, God, call it what
you will—has sometimes nudged and often propelled
me along the right path.

I am in the awesome process of finding the love
and the beauty in conscious living. The furtherance of
my dream is that I may encourage others to tell their
stories and begin to live big. I see it happening now as
I speak to high school students and as I take steps to
write a book, my story.

Our child welfare system in this amazing nation of
Canada is out of sync with the needs of today's society.
Part of my dream is to see the agencies involved, from
child welfare to the courts to police services, revamped
in favor of the protection of youngsters. To do this,
the system must be funded properly and managed by
creative, brilliant, and daring people, who will walk in
where angels truly have not been let loose.

It is not facile to say that our children are our
future; it is unequivocally true. Once the front end of
the machine, the child welfare system, is rebalanced

and working smoothly and creatively, the judicial and police systems will hum along with it.

We need to offer people a safe haven where they can come forward and tell their stories and reveal the secrets that could haunt them until they die. These dark, ugly stories hold us back, leaving us suffering through a life with little self-confidence and causing us to hide in the shadows of our true selves.

We must all come to terms with our stories— whatever they are—and heal. That's a given in life. What is not a given is the assistance of nurturing and protective people along the way.

INTRODUCTION

IN THE SUMMER of 1999, at the age of thirty-five, I was confronted with the undeniable truth that my life wasn't working. My marriage was crumbling. I was headed for divorce for the second time in four years. During those hot summer months, I realized something that had been true for nearly all my life. I was stuck. I was forced to confront a reality I'd been ignoring for as long as I could remember. The pain of being abandoned and abused as a helpless child had left me with deep wounds of guilt and shame.

As a result, I'd lived like a rat trapped in a maze, anxious, desperate, and making the same wrong turns over and over again in a futile search for freedom.

As a younger person, I had tried to cover up the problem with drugs. Thankfully, I quickly realized that the escape they provided only made matters worse. Then I tried relationships. Obviously, that hadn't worked either.

I knew the problem wasn't a lack of intelligence. I was smart enough to do well in business. What I lacked was self-knowledge. I needed someone to help me quit making the same mistakes over and over. So, I went looking for help, real help, not just a Band-Aid to make me feel better. I wanted a permanent solution that would stick. That landed me in the office of a professional counselor named Ellyn. She was a wise woman who was trained to see what I didn't see. What I didn't see, but I was ready to see, was why I was making so many mistakes in my life and that I couldn't seem to get it right.

As I sat in the small waiting room adjacent to her home office, I was nervous but felt a sense of peace. Her home was a century-old stone house set among trees. I'd felt a warm and welcoming feeling even while walking up the sidewalk.

After a few minutes, the office door opened, and I was greeted by a short, round, gray-haired woman, who resembled a kindly aunt or grandmother. I felt safe and trusting.

We sat down, and she began with the usual family history and background questions that therapists ask. I thought, "Here we go again." Same old questions, same old process, and probably the same old result. I challenged her expertise with a question about relationships, trying to cut to the chase. At that Ellyn stood up, walked over, and looked me square in the eyes. She said, "You don't know anything about relationships, and I do, which is why you're here. If you want my help, you better listen."

> **Telling your story does not normalize the harm done to you. It normalizes *you*.**

I respected her for knowing what I was looking for. Within a few sessions, she got beyond my present issue—the divorce—and uncovered the story I had blocked out for too many years. Ellyn's gift was to take me backwards in time to my youth to confront a violent, abusive childhood. My story from the prologue of this book was published in a national newspaper and told on TV and in other books. Many people wonder why I chose to tell a story that was so horrible to endure. The reason is simple. When Ellyn asked me what I needed to do to let go of the terrible weight of guilt and shame, I blurted out, "I want to write my story and go public with it."

So I did.

Talking works. Telling your story does not normalize the harm done to you. It normalizes *you*. After my story was published, I realized I wasn't alone. Many, many others had suffered a similar fate. I came to understand that there wasn't anything wrong with me after all. Wrong had *happened* to me. The guilt and shame I felt existed only because of what I thought about me.

Soon after going public, I began to receive invitations for speaking appearances. People approached me, wanting to know how I was able to move from abuse to freedom. "How did you do it?" they asked. "What's the secret?" I knew what I had done to get unstuck, but I couldn't tell others how to do it. I didn't want anyone to suffer as I had or for as long as I had. I needed to find a way to communicate my road to freedom, not just the details of my abuse.

Sometime later, my then girlfriend told me she was pregnant and that I was going to be a father. We had started out as friends after my second marriage ended, and we hadn't been dating long. I was still struggling with the remnants of my past at a deep, subconscious level. I was still triggered by old wounds that would set me back. The thought of becoming a father added urgency to my quest for healing.

Ellyn once explained to me that I needed to become a parent to "that little boy" who had suffered all those years ago. In other words, I must show myself some love and tenderness. She called it "unconditional positive regard." She said that all the pain, suffering, and mistakes weren't my fault, and they weren't his fault. "What does that little boy need to hear from you?" Ellyn asked. "What do you want him to know based on your years of experience and growth?"

That conversation became a catalyst for the idea of self-parenting. If telling my story had been the first giant step toward my freedom, parenting myself became another.

The third came in May 2014 through my mentor, from whom I learned about the power of mindset and self-image. Through that, I have developed a strong understanding of mindset and how it works for overcoming the shame and trauma of childhood abuse and self-loathing.

Let me be clear about something right up front. I don't have any fancy degrees behind my name. I didn't finish high school. I tried it three times, but I kept quitting and never got past grade ten. I spent years in therapy and saw no change in my life. Same process, same mistakes, same results. But then I figured it out. Nobody can question my process because it worked, and if it can work for me, it can work for you.

The process has enabled me to organize my thinking about what I did and how I did it in a way others can follow to end their struggles, to let go of their own stories.

Getting unstuck and healing is simple! I made it hard, but I discovered why, and I want to show you how simple it can be.

Most people are stuck in an emotional prison, but it's a case of mistaken identity. The real villain is their upbringing and the system that keeps them stuck. The struggle becomes their identity.

Too many people struggle with their past, and they're stuck, which leaves them feeling frustrated and anxious. It impacts their mental well-being and causes them problems at home and at work. They continue to struggle, and worse, they raise children who struggle.

What is a mistaken identity? Your mistaken identity is how you see yourself and the strong perception you have of yourself, which was drilled into you through your conditioning and your upbringing. You see yourself a certain way; you're mistaken about your potential, your qualities, and your gifts. You're convinced you're not worthy of more. You may have low self-esteem. You may be lacking self-confidence in parts of your life and see yourself as unworthy. That's a mistake.

If that sounds familiar, this book is for you. It's a simple pathway to freedom from your emotional prison so you can write a new, empowering story for yourself and live a fulfilling life. This book is a formula for getting unstuck fast.

This book is written as a handbook. Each chapter is only a few pages and is very direct. I don't want you to waste your time like I did. I want to help you get right to the point; I want you to take action and begin experiencing freedom right now.

HOW TO USE THIS BOOK

Each chapter presents a pivotal life lesson, along with changes you can make for incorporating that lesson into your life.

Let me repeat, this is simple. I made it hard. But you don't have to make the same mistake. Learn from my mistakes and follow my instructions. You'll be glad you did.

At the end of each chapter, you will reflect on insights and what you learned from the chapter. Then you will jot down the key points and complete a simple action step. There is a piece of Scripture that I'd like you to meditate on for a few minutes to see if you can connect the lesson to what's on God's mind about you. Even if you don't believe in God, consider what His word says about you.

This simple process, which you can complete in just a few minutes each day, will move you into action. It is your escape plan from the emotional prison you're stuck in.

Don't let this be another "*shelf*-help" book. Take the advice given here. It really works. But you must work too. That's vital. Merely reading this book isn't enough. You need to experience it. After all, you didn't read a book to be taught love. You *experienced* love. And you must experience the release that comes from this process also.

So, make sure to do the exercises. Take action. That's where the magic happens. When you experience the concepts in this book, something happens inside your brain and nervous system, and your mind begins to change. This is how transformation takes place.

Now let me give you the advice Ellyn gave me over twenty years ago. You are not an expert in getting unstuck. I presume if you're reading this, your way is not working. This way does work. So please, commit to this journey for the next thirty days. Read the book daily. Reread it several times. Drill these truths into your mind. Do the exercises. You've wasted enough time and money on solutions that don't work. Deep down, you're hoping this is the answer.

IT IS. LET'S GET STARTED.

If you want to learn from me directly and follow me through this book, go to my website at www.dougdane.com, and I will spend the next month with you as you read.

CHAPTER 01

Stop Judging

Judging a person does not define who they are. It defines who you are.

—Unknown

WHEN YOU STOP judging others, you'll stop judging yourself.

When we are born, we are authentic and filled with love, without judgment. But very early on, we learn to judge. It starts small, and it grows. It grew in you, and it grew in the ones around you who raised you and taught you.

We watched our parents judge people. They criticized the neighbors. They criticized their friends, talking behind people's backs. They criticized each other. And when they raised us, they criticized us. They didn't mean to, but they did.

They told us what was right and wrong and defined what was good and bad. If we got it right, we got praise, love, validation, and approval. But if we got it wrong, then we were judged, criticized, punished, yelled at, ignored, and in my case, hit.

Self-doubt grew within us and we began to judge ourselves. Then we started judging others. We punished ourselves when we didn't measure up, and we looked for validation from others to confirm we were doing things right.

This created our fear of criticism, and we began to worry about what others thought about us. We don't like what we think of ourselves, and we're afraid of what other people think of us. And most of us aren't even aware of it. This fear is further fueled by social media, politics, through fashion and style, and through television and magazines. It's everywhere!

We learned to cover up how we felt or what we thought because we didn't want to be judged. We learned to cover up who we really were, and we fell into line. Then we started to dislike ourselves, maybe even hate ourselves, and we didn't want anyone to know what we thought of ourselves. What would they think of us if they really knew what we were thinking and feeling?

JUDGMENT IS A PANDEMIC, AND IT'S SPREADING.

As an adult and a parent, I see how the cycle is continuing. Many adults are struggling with judgment and the fear of criticism, and they are raising children who are struggling. The parents are struggling to help their struggling children, and they don't know what to do!

> ### Letting go of your past and how you view it is the cure.

I really struggled and got stuck a lot! I judged myself. Who wouldn't? I can imagine how you must feel about yourself. You will see stories throughout this book that you may relate to. Don't judge yourself if you do.

Judgment and fear of criticism causes you to worry. When you worry, it creates anxiety, which leads to depression and maybe worse. Anxiety and depression seem to be the new norm. It seems no one knows what to do. Pills and counseling have become the go-to remedies, but they aren't the cure. Mental health awareness is a popular narrative these days, but it just brings attention to the problem, not the cure. We are treating symptoms, not the cause. Judgment is the cause! Letting go of your past and how you view it is the cure. Learning to like yourself, forgiving yourself, and ridding yourself of worrying about what others think is the cure!

If you realize why you were judged, and you understand why you judge yourself, you can let it go and be free. I'll explain this as we go through this book together.

As a parent, I realized it's not my job to pass along my rules, values, and beliefs that set me up to judge. I'm supposed to rid myself of judgment, so I don't pass it along to my daughter or others in my life. We all run the risk of judging our children and spreading the disease. I still judge other people sometimes. But the difference now is that I catch myself doing it. And when I do catch myself, I stop it, and I remind myself to look for the good in others. For me to see the good in someone else, I must see good in me.

I discovered a cure for self-judgment and fear of criticism. It's a three-step process. The first step is to stop judging others. The second naturally follows: when you stop judging others, you stop judging yourself (or you start judging yourself less), and you feel better about yourself; you become lighter. Third is you become immune to other people's judgment of you. When I became more immune to judgment, the *dis*ease began to ease. When I started treating people better, I started treating myself better. That made me feel free.

It's that simple. Make these steps a habit, and when you do, you'll find that you judge yourself less.

Be careful what you send out because it will come back and hit you in the back of your head. It's called the boomerang effect. As I started to direct more love and acceptance towards others, more love and acceptance came back to me.

When we judge others, it's a reflection of how we feel about ourselves. I discovered there is good in me! The judgments I've made over the years created a *dis*-ease in me that had impacted so many areas of my life. I have now forgiven myself, and I've forgiven those who have hurt me out of their own hurt, judgment, and fear.

When you stop judging others, you stop judging yourself.

I was surprised how simple it was and how quickly things changed for me.

My mission is to help rid others of judgment. If I can get adults to stop judging themselves and others, then they can be freer, and the people they judge will be freer. Then they can free their children from judgment, and they can raise them to be healthier and happier. Their children can grow up to be adults who are healthy and happy and raise children who are also healthy and happy. I figure it'll only take one or two generations to help to reduce enough judgment to create a better world.

■ MEDITATION ■

Do not judge, or you too will be judged. For in the same way you judge others, you will be judged, and with the measure you use, it will be measured to you.

Matthew 7:1–2 NIV

■ INSIGHTS ■

What did you learn from this chapter?

1.

2.

3.

■ ACTION ■

Your first step is to stop judging.

- ■ Make a list of things you judge yourself for.
- ■ Pick one thing from your list; decide you're going to practice letting go of it each day.
- ■ Make a list of the people in your life whom you judge. Pick one person and decide that you are no longer going to judge them, and practice, starting today.

As you practice this first step, pay attention to what you say and think to yourself about others and correct yourself. Look for the good in people. Treat others the way you want to be treated.

CHAPTER 02

You're a Liar

He who permits himself to tell a lie once,
finds it much easier to do it a second and
third time, till at length it becomes habitual.

—Thomas Jefferson

LIES BRING SHAME. Truth sets you free.

My parents lied to each other, they lied to the neighbors to cover up their violence, and they lied to the police when they were called to our home to break up bloody fights. I was taught to lie to cover up what was going on in our home.

My mom and dad fought a lot. Arguments were a daily thing, fueled by the poison of alcohol and inflamed by their own fears and self-loathing. I don't know if my parents were aware of what they were doing to themselves or each other. It was obvious they were

violent alcoholics, and they abused their bodies, pol-
luted their minds, and abused each other. But I don't
think it was obvious to them the damage being done to
themselves or their children.

I was witness to deceit on a regular basis. I was
scolded if I wasn't honest, but I was living with people who lied and who constantly encouraged me to lie.
That's the beginning of me getting lost. My parents were
hypocrites, telling me one thing and doing another.

And like most kids, the second-guessing started
early. It's no wonder I grew up insecure. I didn't have
a sense of right and wrong. I received so many mixed
messages from my parents' behavior, and yet I was
scolded for mine.

Because I was afraid of my parents, I began to lie.
The lies started as "little white lies" so I wouldn't get
in trouble, but then they grew into bigger lies.

We watched our parents lie, and we learned to lie.
We watched them being dishonest with each other,
with others, and with us. We watched them say one
thing and do another, and then we began to do the
same. I began to wonder if what my parents said to me
were lies. I questioned them, and I questioned myself.
More judgment!

LIES AND SECRETS KEEP YOU SICK.

A person can lie so much that they begin to think
it's the truth. The more I lied, the worse I felt about

myself. The shame and regret that comes with lying ate away at me on the inside. Later in life the lies created anxiety and depression, and they caused me to withdraw and detach from myself and others. I believe this is how I began to lose the connection with myself.

At my core I was filled with integrity. We all are but we learn to lie. To protect myself from the abuse, I would lie. To protect myself against loss of love, I would lie. But the lies always catch up to us, and the losses mount and return later at a much higher price.

What's more, lying creates inner-conflict, erodes our self-worth, adds more second-guessing, and breeds more shame. I stacked up my lies like a scorecard against myself. I was a loser.

I couldn't keep all the lies straight. I had been lying for a long time to a lot of people, and I couldn't remember what was true. I wanted to be true to others and to myself but lying was part of who I thought I was.

It was Christmas Day, 2016, and I had finally mustered up the courage to face the truth and tell the truth. I was talking to my friend Pete, trying to work through my paralyzing fear of being honest. As I talked, it hit me that the source of my inner conflict and pain was confusion about who I really was compared to the person I was acting like. It didn't make sense. Was I missing something?

I felt something was missing in me. It was a feeling of emptiness that left a hole in my heart, and I had convinced myself there was something wrong with me. What was missing was a relationship with myself, which I found through understanding my true self better and letting go of my mistaken identity. I was able to do that through a relationship with God first. That was my window to a new relationship with the true me. For others there may be a different way into themselves. When I filled in that hole, I was able to accept the forgiveness He was offering, and then I began to forgive myself.

> **If you don't tell the truth, it causes an internal conflict.**

When I found this connection with myself, I learned to be honest with myself. I learned to be honest with others. Looking back now, I can see how much pain I had caused. I caused pain to those whom I hurt, and I caused myself pain. The truth hurts, but you do heal.

Is it possible you've been lying to yourself and others for too long? I hope this will inspire you to find the courage to be honest with yourself, despite the risks and regardless of what people will think. If you lie because you're worried about what others will think, you'll end up disconnecting from yourself more, and that's destructive. You have nothing to fear from the truth. It would be a shame to keep lying. It would be a shame to try and be anyone else and lie about it.

The truth is positive; a lie is negative.

I challenge you to tell the truth. The truth is positive; a lie is negative. The truth feels good and lies feel bad. How do you want to feel?

Take a risk and connect to yourself and discover who you really are. There's nobody in the universe like you. You're special, and you're a gift. Don't bury it in a lie.

■ MEDITATION ■

Do not lie to each other, since you have taken off your old self with its practices and have put on the new self, which is being renewed in knowledge in the image of its Creator.

Colossians 3:9–10 NIV

■ INSIGHTS ■

What did you learn from this chapter?

1.

2.

3.

■ ACTION ■

Decide right now that you're not going to lie because you're worried about what others think or what they will do. Do not compromise yourself with a lie to cover up your fear of judgment.

- List some things you're not being honest about in your life and how it makes you feel?
- If you could free yourself, what truths would you tell?
- Pick one truth from your list each day and tell the truth.

If you want to be free, be brave and tell the truth. You might be afraid, but you'll become stronger when you do.

CHAPTER 03

Broken Little Boy

Someday you're gonna look back on this moment of your life as such a sweet time of grieving. You'll see that you were in mourning, and your heart was broken, but your life was changing.

—Elizabeth Gilbert, journalist and author

I FELT BROKEN MOST OF MY LIFE!

I had very few memories as a little boy. However, social services' records and police reports describe me as a "happy boy" and someone who was funny. I tried to cover up my pain and fear and the darkness of my homelife through sports and spending time with my friends. Those were fun times with my friends, but I always dreaded going home. When my mom would yell down the street, "Dougie Dane, you get home here right now," I'd be scared.

I never knew what was waiting for me at home. Did I do something wrong? Did I forget to follow the rules? Or was it something else? I was so lost and confused at such an early age. I didn't know what was right or wrong. Everything seemed upside down. I felt so out of place, and I was scared, really scared.

My parents would take their anger out on me, which reinforced my feelings of guilt. It wasn't until much later in life I learned that it's common for abuse victims and children growing up in alcoholic families to take on the blame and the shame. That explained a lot as to why I felt as I did most of my life. Looking back now, I understand why I felt responsible for my parents' darkness and bloody fights, even though I wasn't. But at the time, I thought it must be me.

That's the beginning of feeling broken for most young people because they take on the responsibility for their parents' brokenness. I hope you didn't take on the blame or the shame for your parents' mistakes.

I RECALL FEELING BROKEN EARLY ON.

My parents were broken. They came from a history of violence and alcohol. My birth mom was brought up in it, my adoptive grandparents grew up in it, and like many genetic diseases, it was passed from generation to generation. As an adolescent and a teen, I remember being disgusted and ashamed of my parents. And I felt disgusted with myself.

As I grew older, I saw my dad as a pathetic excuse for a man and father. He was a drunk, he was weak, he was a philanderer, and he beat his wife. He was a terrible example of a man and father.

My mom was dark and sick. She became mentally ill. The shock treatments had taken their toll, and I thought she was *crazy*. She was funny too, but I was still embarrassed by her and some of the antics she would pull. Later, she would beat my dad and treat us poorly.

My grandparents seemed kind, especially my grandmother. But later I was told stories of how my grandfather treated my grandmother. Most of my extended family seemed to drink too much and fight too much.

Violence and booze cause so much damage to people. My situation was no different. I felt like damaged goods.

I broke up our family—or so I thought. I remember the day I called the police, and they came to take my mom away for good. I was angry and scared, but it seemed what needed to be done. I would carry around guilt from that too and was stuck wondering if I caused the family breakup.

Because I felt broken and damaged, I started down the wrong road. Our minds are like a target-seeking missile. Whatever we believe and whatever we think about guides our actions. I was like a broken missile seeking out more broken outcomes. With no real guidance from those who were meant to love and protect me, I was left to find my own way. At first, you'd see the things I did as harmless or typical of a young boy growing up, but for me, everything seemed wrong. I never felt quite right about myself, and I second-guessed myself a lot. Having no benchmark for right or wrong, I was quick to judge and punish myself.

> **Our minds are like a target-seeking missile. Whatever we believe and whatever we think about guides our actions.**

Inside, I felt kindhearted, but there was a dark side to me, and it became a second side of me. Constantly in a battle with my distorted view of right and wrong, I pushed forward in fear.

Although I felt broken growing up, it never broke me. I kept pressing on and so have you. Don't underestimate the power of your spirit. I believe we endure these challenges to strengthen us for a bigger purpose. If you're willing, you could look at your past as preparation for something bigger. There's something waiting for you when you are ready.

■ MEDITATION ■

*The LORD is close to the brokenhearted and saves
those who are crushed in spirit.*

Psalm 34:18 NIV

■ INSIGHTS ■

What did you learn from this chapter?

1.

2.

3.

■ ACTION ■

If you feel broken, maybe something happened to you, or you believe you did something wrong. It's time to change your mind about it!

- List the ways you have felt broken and the reasons why.
- List some things you have blamed yourself for and taken on responsibility for others' mistakes.
- Examine each answer and ask yourself, were those things really your fault?

You'll feel better when you change your mind and your opinion of your past. The key to your future starts by letting go of the past. If you see your past differently, then it's easier to let it go. Too many people want to hold on to the past because they think it defines them. It doesn't!

CHAPTER 04

You Should Be Ashamed

Shame (noun): a painful emotion caused by consciousness of guilt, shortcoming, or impropriety

—Merriam-Webster's Collegiate Dictionary

WHEN OTHERS TRY TO HAND YOU SHAME, REJECT IT.

Shame is toxic. If someone says you should be ashamed of yourself, it's coming from their own shame or their judgment of what you did. Shame is about diminishing one's value or worth in the eyes of others or of themselves.

The truth is you should never feel ashamed for things you've done wrong. Most of the things you've done were based on what you thought was right and wrong, which was formed by rules, values, and beliefs you inherited. Your actions are always because of your beliefs.

In other words, when people say you should be ashamed of yourself, it comes from people trying to bring attention to transgressions or our so-called shortcomings. Some people like to focus and harp on our shortcomings.

Your shame may have come from rules that didn't make any sense. Remember when you were a kid, and you didn't follow the rules? You were told that you should be ashamed of yourself. Maybe your parents should be ashamed of themselves. But like you, they inherited the same rules they were judged by. It's insidious.

I was ashamed of myself. When I was *bad*, my mom would yell at me, "You should be ashamed of yourself." She should have been ashamed of herself for the way she treated me, but it wasn't her fault. It wasn't my fault either if I felt ashamed for some of the things I was doing.

NOBODY SHOULD CARRY AROUND THE WEIGHT OF SHAME.

As I grew up, a dark side seemed to be growing in me. Witnessing the violence was taking its toll on me. I remember when I was seven, I lived in a foster home on a farm with a Mennonite family for the summer. My dad had been arrested for beating my mom. The police took him away, and my mom was hospitalized for weeks to treat her injuries; we were taken from our home by the police and social services and placed in foster care.

> **Guilt should not be carried on, and if you do carry it on, it breeds more shame.**

One time we went to a neighboring farm for the day, and my brother and I and our foster brother were left alone to entertain ourselves. I felt so ashamed about what we did that day. We chased chickens around the yard and slaughtered them by kicking them and stomping on them.

I was ashamed, and I felt sick about what I did. I felt guilty, of course, and that's healthy in the moment because it's getting your attention to something you've done wrong. But guilt should not be carried on, and if you do carry it on, it breeds more shame. But I was seven years old, and I didn't have anyone to help me address things I was doing wrong or what I felt guilty about. That fueled more shame. I couldn't be honest about what I did because I felt guilty and ashamed. I was always worried about the punishment I would get because I was constantly being punished.

Luckily, the family fostering me cared about me. They cared more about me than I did about myself.

That saved me in some ways. When I was returned home that fall, things got worse for me and escalated.

When I think of the men who sexually abused me, I don't think they should be ashamed of themselves. They were guilty of the charges, and they were convicted, but I'm saddened by their stories, which caused them to do what they did to me. It's a shame that they turned out that way.

Our social system can breed shame. Victims of child abuse feel ashamed. I remember when the police detectives knocked on my door one night. I had just been returned to my home by the pedophile who had kidnapped me in order to avoid police arrest. The detectives took me down into my basement to interview me privately. They showed me photos of me and the men and asked me what I knew about the men who had abused me. They scared me, and I felt threatened. They left quicky and left me alone with my guilt and shame. My father couldn't do anything or offer anything. I wish someone had just said, "It's okay Doug; it wasn't about you. There's nothing wrong with you. Don't be ashamed."

But I was offered nothing. I was left with numbness and shame.

Weeks later I sat in the hallway of the courthouse waiting to be called to testify. The time never came, and I never had to testify. I remember feeling scared but also wanting to speak up. I was fifteen and a minor, so my identity was protected. That inflamed my mistaken identity and my shame. The criminals at the time were the men who had abused me, but I was left in an emotional prison, and I felt like a victim.

> ## I'm no longer ashamed of myself, and neither should you be.

The system tries to protect innocent minors, but I believe it only furthers their guilt and shame. The system makes them feel like something is wrong with them. It's wrong that children are abused, but in my case, it was wrong that I felt ashamed. Now that's not the case in every situation, but I believe we need to stop breeding toxic shame.

Where does shame end? Where does it begin? That's what we need to change.

I'm no longer ashamed of myself, and neither should you be. Whatever you have done in your life that you're ashamed of, perhaps you paid the price already. Perhaps you've punished yourself enough, and it's time to let it go.

Shame can kill your dreams, and it can kill love. It's also causing people to kill themselves. It's a shame people feel shame through no fault of their own and they are struggling because of it.

■ MEDITATION ■

Therefore, there is now no condemnation for those who are in Christ Jesus.

Romans 8:1 NIV

■ INSIGHTS ■

What did you learn from this chapter?

1.

2.

3.

■ ACTION ■

It's time to let go of your shame. You have nothing to be ashamed of. Whatever you are ashamed about, you are forgiven. It's not your fault anymore.

- List things you feel ashamed of and tear up the list.
- Thank God for being forgiven and vow to leave your shame where it belongs, in the past.

Your shame isn't serving you. It's only holding you back. Your shame might be contagious, and you don't want others around you to suffer. Don't worry; there is more to come on how to do this, so stay with me.

CHAPTER 05

What Are You Hiding?

Our deepest fear is not that we are inadequate. Our deepest fear is that we are powerful beyond measure. . . . You are a child of God. Your playing small does not serve the world.

—Marianne Williamson, author

WHEN YOU REALIZE PEOPLE DON'T CARE, YOU WON'T HAVE TO HIDE.

Recently I discovered another part of my mistaken identity that was holding me back from pursuing my dreams and writing this book. I've held back for way too long because I was fearful of what others would think. Even when I did show up and speak up and got positive feedback, I would still hold back.

Someone close to me asked, "Why do you think you are hiding? What are you afraid of? Where did the fear come from?"

When I was young, I had to hide to stay safe, so hiding has been safe for me. When I was little, and my parents were drunk and fighting, or my mom would yell out in her ugly, loud slur, "Dougie Dane, where are you?" I'd hide to stay safe. When I did something wrong, I'd hide to stay safe from getting "the strap" (a leather belt). When I escaped the madness in our home to the respite of a neighbor's house, they would hide me to keep me safe.

I used to hide in the spruce bushes in front of our house. They were thick and tall and a good place to hide. The bushes were right under the kitchen window where my mom used to yell for me. It was like her perch, and it was embarrassing hearing her yell ring through the neighborhood, but worse was fearing she might find me.

Coping mechanisms get built in at an early age. No child should have to hide to stay safe, and certainly no adult should have to stay hidden from their calling or purpose because they're afraid to come out of the dark and into the light.

Hiding things to stay safe became a habit for me. When I faced conflict, or when I made a mistake in work or in my personal relationships, I'd keep it hidden. People would ask, "Doug, what are you hiding?" My answer was always the same: "Nothing!" And so the hiding continued.

When you keep things hidden, you have more lies to cover up. Each time I covered things up I'd give myself a hard time. The self-talk continued, and now I had more to hide.

YOU'VE GOT NOTHING TO HIDE!

I read somewhere that if you tell the truth about everything, to everyone, all the time, you'll never have to worry about what others will think, and you won't have to hide. I hope you're not hiding like I was hiding. If you are hiding, stay with me.

My mentor kept asking me, "Doug, why are you hiding?" I'd say, "I'm not hiding." But he'd call me out saying, "Yes you are!" "I'm not," I would repeat, but I was hiding, and he knew it. He said, "Doug, you'll stop worrying about what others think of you when you realize they very rarely do. Stop hiding!"

When I first started speaking up about my story, I used to hide. Before I had to speak, I'd hide in the bathroom. When I'm nervous or anxious, I sweat. My feet sweat; my palms sweat, and they become clammy and cold. I would get so nervous that my shirt would be soaking wet under my arms. I would go to the bathroom and grab paper towels to scrub and dry the wetness from my arms. I'd bend over in a funny position to run the hand dryer on my shirt, or I'd hide in my hotel room and blow-dry my sweaty shirt. Then I would cover it up with my jacket, hoping it wouldn't show. It's funny to me now because I'm the only one who noticed or cared. I was so afraid that people would notice, so I would hide it.

My partner saw that I was hiding, and she kept affirming I should stop hiding. Finally, I accepted that, and I started to affirm that being in the public eye is good and safe for me. Showing up and speaking up is good for me.

The truth is, I have nothing to hide. And neither do you.

I made up my mind that I wasn't going to hide anymore. The truth is, I have nothing to hide. And neither do you. Don't be afraid of what people will think; they're not thinking of you anyway. They're busy worrying about themselves and what they're hiding. It's just plain wrong that we keep the truth about ourselves hidden from the world.

The things that I hid, and the things I hid from, no longer need to hinder me. I can't change the past, and I can't control the future. We hide things from our past out of fear of what others think, and we hide what we think and feel because we're afraid of the future or what others will say and do.

The more I distance myself from worrying what others think or what they will do, the freer I have become, and the better I feel. There's nothing for me to hide from, and the same goes for you!

If you don't break the habit of hiding, it will stop you from living the life you're meant to live and becoming who you're meant to be. Stop hiding and start living.

▪ MEDITATION ▪

For all that is secret will eventually be brought into the open, and everything that is concealed will be brought to light and made known to all.

Luke 8:17 NLT

▪ INSIGHTS ▪

What did you learn from this chapter?

1.

2.

3.

■ ACTION ■

If you want to stop hiding, take an honest look at *what* you're hiding. If you and I were sitting down talking as if we were close, trusted friends, tell me what are you hiding?

- Make a list of the things you've been hiding from others.
- Cross off the ones that are making you feel small.
- Decide on one thing you're going to do to stop hiding and practice showing up each day.

If you keep hiding, you'll feel lost until you find yourself. The fastest way to the truth about yourself is to *tell* the truth about yourself. I know it seems scary, but I'm telling you, you don't need to hide anymore.

CHAPTER 06

There's Nothing Wrong with You

I know for sure that what we dwell on is what we become.

—Oprah Winfrey

You will not be free until you believe you are free.

What's wrong with me? That was a question I was asking myself over and over most of my life. How about you? Do you find yourself asking that question? I'd ask that all the time and then shake my head in frustration, disgusted with myself. I wasn't the only one shaking their head, asking me what was wrong with me. Others did too.

How did this start? From an early age I remember my parents punishing me and criticizing me because I didn't get things right. When I didn't do what I was told, my mom would yell at me in her drunken stupor: "What the heck is wrong with you?"

When she would ask that, I wouldn't have an answer, but it became a question I took on and carried forward into my adult life. I really believed there was something wrong with me. I could feel it. I was nervous, anxious, and scared, and I was making all kinds of mistakes and breaking the rules. There must be something wrong with me. But still, I never got an answer to that question.

I was born on October 30, the day before Halloween. In Canada where I grew up, the day before Halloween was called devil's night. Kids would go out and throw eggs at people's homes, smash pumpkins, and vandalize the neighborhoods. When I was little, my mom called me "a little devil." My adopted brother was born the day before Valentine's Day, and he was "a little angel." I fulfilled that "devil" role. I was a "bad" kid and got into a lot of trouble.

As I grew older, I kept wondering, *What's wrong with me?*

If you've been asking yourself that question, you probably haven't gotten an answer either. The reason you haven't gotten an answer is because there's nothing wrong with you! Now you might say, "Doug, if you only knew what I've done!" Let me tell you, you wouldn't have done what you did if you were brought up believing something different about yourself. That's what you must get straight in your mind. The main reason you did things wrong is because of what you were told when you were little.

> **There is nothing wrong with you. The only thing that's wrong is what you believe about yourself.**

The reason you feel like there is something wrong with you comes from years of believing lies told to you about yourself that were never true. There is nothing wrong with you. The only thing that's wrong is what you believe about yourself, which caused you to do what you did, and that makes you feel like something is wrong with you.

After years of struggle and abuse and then self-abuse, trying to mask the pain of feeling "off," I finally figured it out. There's nothing wrong with me! That's why I never got an answer to that question.

SAY IT OUT LOUD: "THERE'S NOTHING WRONG WITH ME!"

It took me a long time to come to that conclusion. I had made so many mistakes that I believed there must be something wrong with me. The thing I felt the worst about was that I always cheated in my relationships.

I was a good person, but I kept doing things wrong. I had become a philanderer like my adoptive father. That was wrong.

> **Regardless of how you came to believe there's something wrong with you, it's time to drop it and let it go.**

I liked the attention I would get from women because it gave me temporary validation, but the self-loathing after the fact was debilitating. I kept beating myself up for my mistakes, and the shame piled up. I kept doing things that confirmed there must be something wrong with me. And the guilt and judgment that came, consequently, only made it worse.

My mistaken identity came from the repetitive physical and emotional abuse I was subjected to. It was a constant rhythm, like a beating, which was a drum drilled into me by the adults. Regardless of how you came to believe there's something wrong with you, it's time to drop it and let it go. It really is that simple. By now you're starting to see how your mistaken identity has deceived you. In your heart, you know you're a good person. You know there's nothing wrong with you.

I'm finally free, and I no longer carry on the habits of a broken man. There's nothing wrong with me. I lived with a mistaken identity. I'm a good man. I'm a good father. I'm a good partner. I'm filled with integrity, and I'll never cheat on myself again. My cheating caused me to cheat myself out of a better life. I cheated myself out of a better life because I believed things that weren't true about me, and I made a lot of mistakes. Thinking something is wrong with you is cheating on yourself. I'll always be true to myself from now on.

If you're struggling, it's time you learned the truth. The truth is, there is nothing wrong with you. The only thing wrong is what you believe about yourself. The truth is, you've been lying to yourself and others about who you really are. The truth is, you bought into things that weren't true, and you lost your way.

■ MEDITATION ■

Do not judge, and you will not be judged. Do not condemn, and you will not be condemned. Forgive, and you will be forgiven.

Luke 6:37 NIV

■ INSIGHTS ■

What did you learn from this chapter?

1.

2.

3.

▪ ACTION ▪

If your young child came to you and asked, "Mommy, Daddy, what's wrong with me?" What would you do? You'd reassure them of the truth and tell them there's nothing wrong with them. You need to do the same for yourself.

- Make a list of the things you think are wrong with you.
- Where did those things come from? It's like asking your child, "Who told you that, honey? Where did you hear that?"
- Strike out all the things that aren't true.

You may find it a bit challenging to face the truth. The resistance you feel is coming from a lie that you believe. Give yourself a chance. There is good in you. Let it rise up. You are a good person, and you deserve good.

CHAPTER 07

Poison

Ask no questions and you'll be told no lies.

—Charles Dickens, from *Great Expectations*

You may have been poisoned.

Eat your vegetables. An apple a day keeps the doctor away. If you don't brush your teeth, they'll fall out. Remember those urgings? What are some of the things your parents fed you?

I think of some of the things I had to swallow, literally. My mom would make me drink Buckley's cough syrup. Their tagline was, "It tastes lousy, but it works." It tasted lousy, and it didn't work.

There were a lot of things the adults made you swallow, which tasted awful and didn't work. I'm not talking about food or medicine; I'm talking about all the things that weren't true that they jammed down your throat. It was the same things their parents fed them, and they passed it along to you.

All the poison that was fed to me caused the *dis-ease* in me. It wasn't long before I started feeling unwell and started thinking, "Something's wrong with me."

I remember when I was struggling through my sexual abuse. The men in the ring of pedophiles convinced me that their abuse was love. To convince me their abuse was "normal," they would show me excerpts from a book that explained that experiencing sex with another male was normal. The book didn't say that it was normal for a thirteen-year-old boy to be exploring sex with his fifteen-year-old friend or with a twenty-six-year-old man.

I remember the first time. The first man to reel my friend and me in was a manager at a Radio Shack store. We would skip school and hang out at his store. He invited us to a party at his house one night, and when we arrived, there was no party. We were greeted by his wife who was going out for the evening, and we were left alone with this man. He convinced my friend to go upstairs to his room. As I sat quietly on my own, I knew what was going on upstairs. When it was over, we both walked home without saying a word, knowing what we did was wrong but too ashamed to speak of it.

It was a strange and confusing time for me because it felt good physically, but emotionally I was left with a feeling of guilt and shame. Talk about poison. I felt so bad about myself and the secrets I was carrying, it started to show up in my physical body. I suffered from skin problems and gastric ulcers. Sometimes I could barely walk. The pain was too much to bear, and I would lie down on the ground in the fetal position until the pain subsided.

THE POISON CAN OFFER WISDOM.

You don't have to look at what happened to you as a bad thing. I decided I was going to start over, and I was going to change my mind. I decided it wasn't anyone's fault. Not my adoptive parents', not my birth mom's, not my abusers', nor anyone else's. I took responsibility for my life. I put my stake in the ground and formed a new credo to live by.

> ### The beauty of life kept me going and kept me alive.

Amongst all the poison there was also beauty. I didn't see it at the time, but the beauty of life kept me going and kept me alive. Peacocks can feed on poisonous plants, and they have the ability to convert the poison to helpful compounds that enhance their feather colors and their beauty. Human beings have a unique ability to transform negative things into wisdom and thrive. But it is up to us to make that choice.

One of the most inspiring examples of this human capacity is Viktor Frankl, author of the book *Man's Search for Meaning.* He survived imprisonment in a Nazi concentration camp. I encourage you to read his book.

When I started to see my abuse as a gift, I was lighter. That was a turning point.

I eliminated all the poisonous people in my life. I fired my friends. I went inside myself to get to know *me* and what I had learned and taken in over the years. I found a new "Kool-Aid" to drink, and it tastes good.

Some stories are more severe than others, but the outcome is much the same. We're left with this bad taste in our mouth and gut-wrenching feelings inside.

You can get rid of this "poison." There is an antidote. You don't have to believe everything you were told. You can reject some of the things you were fed. You can choose what you want to believe.

No more poison, only wisdom!

■ MEDITATION ■

A good tree produces good fruit, and a bad tree produces bad fruit. A good tree can't produce bad fruit, and a bad tree can't produce good fruit.

Matthew 7:17–18 NLT

■ INSIGHTS ■

What did you learn from this chapter?

1.

2.

3.

■ ACTION ■

Aren't you sick and tired of being sick and tired?

- ■ What poison did you swallow?
- ■ What's something that happened to you that makes you sick?
- ■ How can you look at it differently? What's the wisdom or gift in it?

If you look at things differently, you can see yourself differently. Just because some things made you feel sick, doesn't mean you need to stay sick. Your suffering comes from your perception of what happened to you.

CHAPTER 08

The Big Con

You are remembered for the rules you break.
—General Douglas MacArthur

DON'T BELIEVE EVERYTHING YOU'RE TOLD.

In the movie *The DaVinci Code*, there is a scene in which the lead character sees words scrawled across a painting: "So dark the con of man." There has been a big con, though it's not the one referred to in that movie.

I remember my mentor saying to me, "There are God-made rules and man-made rules. The man-made rules are always changing, and you'll never measure up, Doug, so stop trying. Which rules are you following?"

That really hit me! The man-made rules I had been handed were messed up. My adoptive parents were raised in a fog of booze and fighting, and they passed their adopted rules along to me. It's no wonder I was confused; the rules were confusing, and nobody was following them anyway. I was adopted, and then I adopted the rules that my parents had adopted from their parents. Do you see the irony?

> **The big con is that we are locked into beliefs that we hold dear and strong, yet they don't feel right to us.**

The big con is that we've been handed rules by family, schools, churches, communities, and cultures, but it's all made up. Everyone is playing the game differently. The big con is that we are locked into beliefs that we hold dear and strong, yet they don't feel right to us. It feels like we were conned.

Think about it. You are a unique individual; there is nobody like you in the entire world, and there never will be. But you're not supposed to act differently or be unique.

The big con is that we are expected to follow man-made rules and fall into line with the masses, but the rules are different in other parts of the world. Conformity is a requirement pushed upon us. With access to news and events all over the world, we pick up information, we form judgments, and the rules get blurry. What is right and wrong? Who decides? The current leaders, celebrities, so-called gurus, or social media influencers?

DO YOU EVER WONDER WHY YOU REBELLED WHEN YOU WERE YOUNG?

Do you ever ask yourself why things don't feel right to you? When you were young, you sensed something was off track. You didn't know what the right track was, but something was definitely off track. Many of the rules that you were expected to follow didn't make sense, and the people drilling the rules into you were hypocrites because they didn't follow them either.

You started to fight back and question the authorities. You didn't have any power, so you were pushed down, and you retreated. In your early teens you tried again, and likely you were dismissed as being disrespectful or a "problem." You caved again, and your questions came back again.

When you didn't follow the rules, you got punished. How did that make you feel? Many people have been raised with a low self-image and an inferiority complex because they were conned to believe they weren't good enough.

I work with people from all over the world, born into different cultures and religions, who speak different languages. When I work with them, sometimes I think to myself, *You were born into the wrong family and the wrong culture.* They don't belong. They feel out of place. The rules don't sit well with them. They are struggling with the rules they were handed, and because of fear of judgment and criticism, they struggle, they suppress themselves, or they hide. Some break free. And some don't survive.

Young people are in trouble! They are more confused than ever, but they think they have all the answers. The internet is filled with misinformation, and it's fed through their phones and social media. Because the adults are confused, the young people don't trust them, and they turn to peers for direction. They are being conned too.

> **Your mistaken identity was caused by you being conditioned to accept rules, values, and beliefs, even if they didn't feel right to you or suit you.**

When I was twenty-three, and my dad died, I went to the bank to close his accounts and empty his safety deposit box. In it I found my adoption order, and my real name was covered up by white tape, which had yellowed over the years. I held it to the light, and I found my birth name. I remember thinking, I'm not a "Jeffrey".

I was able to track down non-identifying information about my birth parents. I remember sitting down to read it over dinner one night. I had made a nice meal, and as I read my birth father's family background, I was sickened. He suffered from mental illness and had been in and out of institutions. The record states that he had been described at a mental clinic as being attention seeking and somewhat of a liar. At the time, it made me sick because I wondered if this would be my future. We con ourselves into believing things.

If I stayed in the family I was born into, I'd be a different person, and I'd be living a different life. Based on my birth parents' stories, things could've been worse. I could have been dropped into any family, and depending on where that was, I would have been conned into believing something very different. I was brought up in my adoptive family, and I wasn't so lucky, but now I feel lucky because my perspective is different. I feel free because I'm free to make up my own rules and I don't have to be ruled by others' rules.

Your mistaken identity was caused by you being conditioned to accept rules, values, and beliefs, even if they didn't feel right to you or suit you. There isn't anything wrong with you; the only thing wrong is that you've been conned into accepting man-made rules set by other people, but they don't work for you.

Break free and make up your own rules. Don't be conned. Have the courage to change the rules. If you're going to follow rules, follow the rules of nature and the God-made rules (but not religion).

■ MEDITATION ■

Don't let anyone capture you with empty philoso-phies and high-sounding nonsense that come from human thinking and from the spiritual powers of this world, rather than from Christ.

Colossians 2:8 NLT

■ INSIGHTS ■

What did you learn from this chapter?

1.

2.

3.

■ ACTION ■

Life is a game, but it's your life. Play a game with yourself, and make up your own rules. Don't follow everyone else's. Don't worry, you won't have to worry about other people's rules after finishing this book.

- ■ What were you conned into believing?
- ■ List some of the made-made rules you adopted, which you don't agree with now.
- ■ Write your own rules to replace them.

You may as well make up your own rules because the rules are going to change anyway.

CHAPTER 09

You're an Imitation

Imitation (noun): the assumption of
behavior observed in other individuals

—Merriam Webster's Collegiate Dictionary

THERE'S NOTHING BETTER THAN THE ORIGINAL.

Whether you like it or not, you were brought up to be an imitation. When you were little, you started imitating your parents. You spoke the way they spoke; you ate what they ate; you copied your dad shaving or your mom cooking. Whatever you observed, you learned to copy. All you wanted was to be loved and accepted, so you started to copy them to be accepted by them.

Because of the judgment and the rules imposed on you, conformity became the next thing you succumbed to. Not wanting to upset anything or anyone and not wanting to stand out, you fell in line and continued to mimic and imitate the adults.

No wonder people feel fake sometimes. That feeling you had growing up, wondering what was feeling "off" with you, was because you were handed a mask and told to wear it.

From very early on, things didn't feel right to you. You watched your parents argue and worry and struggle with their own mistaken identity. As you learned from them, you learned to cover things up. *Don't tell people what you're thinking. Keep your feelings to yourself. Don't speak unless spoken too. Be honest.* Yet most people weren't.

> **You're an imitation because you learned to pretend to be someone you're not.**

Are you confused? I sure was.

Your mistaken identity was created from being taught to imitate or copy others. When you were able to think for yourself, you started worrying about what others thought of you. We say we're all individuals, yet we were told we should be the same as everyone else to be sure we don't "stand out." You're an imitation because you learned to pretend to be someone you're not so you'd be liked, get invited to parties, be included with the cool people, get picked for the team, or whatever else that made you feel like you "fit in" when you were young.

You were afraid of being judged. How could you ever be the real you when you were raised to be so concerned about what others thought? Many people say they struggle with imposter syndrome. It's no wonder. You're not an imposter just because you're acting like one.

STOP FAKING IT. IT'S KILLING YOU.

I remember a time when I faked it. When I was in middle school, running was an escape for me. I was running from lots of things in my life, so cross-country running became an escape. And like anything that I set my mind to, I got good at it. Soon I was the fastest runner in my school. I won the school track meet and qualified for the county track meet.

For the first time, my dad showed up at the meet, and I was so happy he was watching in the stands. I remember turning the final corner of the 800-meter race. I was in second place, and I knew I could beat the leader. As I turned the final corner, I saw my dad in the stands, and I fell. I hit the dirt track, looked up, and saw my win turn into a loss.

I faked it. I faked the fall to get attention. In fact, I faked the cause. My coach and others ran out to see if

I was okay, and I faked my explanation. I faked that I had a pain in my chest that caused me to "black out." I continued to carry the lie on through multiple medical appointments and tests. There was no way I was going to tell the truth. I faked the whole thing to get attention and make myself feel better about myself. I began imitating a victim and I got really good at it. Turns out it wasn't so good for me.

The key to freedom is to be yourself.

If you're reading this book, you may be searching for your authentic self. You're searching for a feeling of peace and contentment within yourself. The key to freedom is to be yourself. Take off the mask and show the world who you really are. Stop faking it and worrying what others think of you.

Stop imitating others to be liked. Be yourself, that's a heck of a lot easier.

■ MEDITATION ■

So we have stopped evaluating others from a human point of view. At one time we thought of Christ merely from a human point of view. How differently we know him now! This means that anyone who belongs to Christ has become a new person. The old life is gone; a new life has begun!

2 Corinthians 5:16-17 NLT

■ INSIGHTS ■

What did you learn from this chapter?

1.

2.

3.

■ ACTION ■

If you want to free yourself, you're going to have to stop pretending to be somebody you're not.

- Name three ways you pretend to be somebody you're not.
- What's one thing you can stop doing that makes you feel like an imitation?
- Do that and you'll feel free. Then repeat it each day.

It's so much easier to be yourself. Think of how much you struggle when you're pretending. Think of how much easier it would be if you could just be yourself. Don't worry about the consequences. If you live the truth, the truth will take care of everything else.

CHAPTER 10

It's Easier to Be Yourself

Take no thought of who is right or wrong or who is better than. Be not for or against.

—Bruce Lee

WHEN YOU ACCEPT YOUR TRUE SELF, YOU'LL BE TRULY FREE.

For most of my life I was struggling to be somebody I wasn't. I kept trying to force the idea of who I should be. When people say, "You can be or do anything you want," that's not completely true. The truth is, you need to understand who and what you are and accept both your strengths and limitations. You can be or do anything you want within the limits of your true self.

You are always aspiring to be a better version of yourself; it's built into you. It's in your nature to want to do better. It's human to want to be better and do better. But the problem is, society has a distorted view on what this means and how it works, and the distortion is being fueled by social media, misinformation, and the self-help industry.

By comparing yourself with others it might feel like something's wrong with you. When we compare ourselves to others it doesn't make us feel very good. We can end up feeling inferior or jealous or even defeated. And when you don't feel good, it's easy to think there's something wrong or blame your circumstances for your feelings of inferiority. Either way you give away your agency over your life. Most mental *dis*ease is caused more by the distorted opinion people have of themselves than by the things going on in their life. They would feel a lot more at ease if they weren't struggling to be someone they're not. Trying to be something we're not can cause anxiety and depression.

You've got to get clear on who your true self is, the self that God created in His image, and separate that from the self you think you must become in order to be happy or accepted.

You'll be a lot happier if you accept yourself as you are rather than fighting to become something you're not—and then punishing yourself or others around you because you can't become who *you think you should become*. Too many people are trying to be who others want them to be or who they think they should be in order to feel loved, validated, and accepted.

I love this from Thomas Troward's essay "Yourself" in his book *The Hidden Power*: "It must surely be easier to be oneself than to be something or somebody else. Yet that is what so many are constantly trying to do; the self that is their own is not good enough for them, and so they are always trying to go one better than what God has made them, with endless strain and struggle as the consequence."[1] That really struck me when I first read it, and almost instantly I felt emotional relief.

> **You'll be a lot happier if you accept yourself as you are rather than fighting to become something you're not.**

Last night I was waiting in line at customs at the Toronto airport, and it was very busy. There were huge lines, and the customs area was swelling with people coming into Canada from all over the world. As the line slowly snaked its way around, I noticed all the different

---

1. Thomas Troward, *The Hidden Power And Other Papers Upon Mental Science*, (New York: Robert M. McBride & Company, 1922), 99-104.

people. I noticed the obvious things, like there were no two people who looked the same. They were different shapes and sizes and colors. They all were wearing something different. I noticed their shoes. Out of thousands of people, I didn't see one person wearing the same shoes as someone else.

WE'RE ALL DIFFERENT, YET WE'RE CONCERNED ABOUT BEING THE SAME.

There's nothing more damaging to your self-confidence than comparing yourself to others. When you can identify with who your true self is and accept yourself as you are, without attaching your failures and mistakes to yourself, you will be free.

My biggest challenge was to be myself in relationships. I tried so hard to be someone who could attract the other person to me, so I would pretend to be something or someone I wasn't. And then if I did attract them, I was in trouble because now I had the worry that they might find out I wasn't who I pretended to be. It's no wonder I struggled. I put myself under a lot of pressure. Then I began to lie to cover up the truth of who I wasn't.

I decided to let go of striving to be somebody I was not. That's been a lot easier and since then life has gotten easier.

■ MEDITATION ■

As the Father has loved me, so have I loved you. Abide in my love.

John 15:9 ESV

■ INSIGHTS ■

What did you learn from this chapter?

1.

2.

3.

■ ACTION ■

If you would just "be yourself," you'd feel a lot better about yourself, and life would be a lot easier.

- Make a list of all the people you compare yourself to; how do you compare?
- What things would you change in your life if you could be yourself?
- List all the ways you would feel better about your life if you could be yourself.

Being yourself might feel a little scary at first because you've been living the other way for so long. Don't worry; everything will work out. You can't go wrong being yourself.

CHAPTER 11

It Wasn't Because of Me!

Don't take anything personally.

—don Miguel Ruiz, author of *The Four Agreements*

Bad things happen to good people.

Growing up I missed out on a lot that we now know young children need. I didn't get the connection I needed when I was young.

I didn't get the love and validation I needed. I had to go searching for them elsewhere. I didn't get direction and guidance when I got stuck or lost, so I went looking for someone to listen to me, and I ended up in the hands of a ring of pedophiles. I suffered for a long time with a case of mistaken identity.

My counselor, Ellyn, introduced me to the book *The Four Agreements* by don Miguel Ruiz. She insisted that she would help me only if I started to study and apply the principles in the book. That book literally saved my life!

The second "agreement" in the book says, "Don't take anything personally." That was very hard for me because, for the longest time, I took everything personally. When people would say and do things that hurt me or triggered past hurt, I'd take it very personally.

> **I let go of the disgust and loathing toward myself and the men who had abused me.**

Surprisingly as I started to practice this new agreement, I began to understand that the abuse I had suffered wasn't because of me. Because of my perspective on my adoption, it helped me to see that any young boy could have landed in that home, and I could've ended up somewhere else. The abuse wasn't because of me! It simply happened to me. If it wasn't me, it would have been another little boy. I don't mind being a former victim because I saved another.

That was a huge letting go, and I began to practice not taking anything about my abuse personally. I let go of the pain and anger toward my parents. I let go of the disgust and loathing toward myself and the men who had abused me. I accepted the idea that it had nothing to do with me.

I hired a private investigator to help piece my story together. He helped me find police records. He tried to find the address of the man who abused me the most—his name is Randy—and he tried to track him down.

The investigator asked me why I wanted to find him. I told him I wanted to sit down with him and find out what happened to him. I wanted to help him. I wanted to let him know he was okay. I didn't want him to take personally what happened to him, which caused him to do what he did to me and others. I never found him, but if I had, I would have hugged him and tried to help him. I know this is the only way to stop the cycle.

> **It's not about you. It simply happened to you.**

I don't take my abuse personally any longer. I don't take my adoption personally. I don't take the mistakes I made in my past personally. I try not to take anything personally anymore because what others say and do (even to me) is not about me. Sometimes I still do take things personally, but I keep practicing this agreement. Thank you, Ellyn, for pushing me, and thank you don Miguel Ruiz for your book and your wisdom.

If you're reading this, my hope is you will let go of your past hurts and mistakes. I hope you won't take it personally. It's not about you. It simply happened to you. I hope you can let go of what you think you need that you didn't get, that you should've had when you were young. It's too late. You can't get it back, and you don't need it.

I wasted so many years trying to get back what I didn't get until I finally made up my mind that none of it was about me, and I don't need what I thought I needed. Let it go. Let it all go!

■ MEDITATION ■

And Jesus said, "Father, forgive them, for they know not what they do."

Luke 23:34 ESV

■ INSIGHTS ■

What did you learn from this chapter?

1.

2.

3.

▪ ACTION ▪

If you want to free yourself from your shame, guilt, and resentment, don't take anything personally.

- ▪ Name the things that happened to you that made you think it was about you.
- ▪ Forgive each person for their shortcomings, and let go of the negative memory.

If you keep making this about you, you will remain a victim and stay stuck. If you change the story you're telling, you'll change how you view it, and your life will change. This could be the turning point for you. It sure was for me. After this chapter and exercise, you don't need to talk about it or even think about it anymore.

When you're done with this book, go get *The Four Agreements* by Don Miguel Ruiz, take inventory of your agreements, and then replace them with the four agreements.

CHAPTER 12

I've Had Enough!

Enough is enough, and it's time for change.

—Owen Hart, Canadian professional wrestler

I<small>T'S OKAY TO GET PISSED OFF.</small>

I got so sick of second-guessing myself and feeling the way I was feeling about myself. Maybe you're feeling that now or you remember how you felt when you got to that point. If you keep holding onto your story, and if you keep living like a victim, it's time to say *enough is enough.*

I wasted so much time, I made things so hard, and I thought getting better was going to be very difficult. Well, I got exactly what I expected. But when I broke free of my emotional prison, I realized how easy it was to escape.

I have had some serious conversations with myself. I got sick of being a victim, and when my "poor me" ego kicks in, I kick its butt. I'll sit down and have a chat with myself: "Now Doug, listen up, enough is enough; you're better than this, and you're not going to sit around whining and moping and being a victim." Take responsibility or you'll stay stuck.

It's not as hard as you think it is to break out.

If you stepped outside your current situation and looked at yourself from an outsider's point of view, you would see yourself much differently. You'd see it's not as hard as you think it is to break out. You just need to decide that enough is enough, and you must stop making excuses and creating alibis to justify why you're stuck. Once you do that, you will start to see a way out. As my friend Jenny Kuspira says, "Decision is the door."

If I sat down with you and got a picture of your current situation, I could see your path to freedom. If I can see it, you can see it, but you must be willing to look for it. And I know you can feel it. I know you know that you are better than the way you're being treated and the way you're treating yourself.

Don't buy into all the mental junk you feed yourself to justify why you're stuck. You would never be where you are if you believed something different about yourself or if you were handed a different identity.

If you've thought about stepping up and breaking free, but you have fears and doubts, that's normal. If you want to know what's right or wrong, just pay attention to your feelings.

Your mistaken identity (ego) defines itself by the past, and any hint of a change is a threat. Your ego isn't a "thing" but for the purpose of making the point, I call your false self, ego. The comfort zone is where it wants to stay. It doesn't like change or want change and since it defines itself by the past, if the future is uncertain, it doesn't like it and will resist change any way it can. Nobody wants to be changed—especially your ego. But your ego is wrong about you.

BE TOUGH WITH YOURSELF AND DEMAND MORE OF YOURSELF, BUT DON'T BE HARD ON YOURSELF.

One of the biggest mistakes I made was being hard on myself. And for good reason. I used to say if I revealed all the things I've done in my life, I wouldn't have anybody in my life. Now, that's not true, but I was afraid of that. I've been hard on myself for most of my life. I learned how to be that way from the people who were hard on me. This caused me to see myself in a way where I didn't like myself, so I didn't treat myself well. That caused me to treat others poorly.

It was my daughter who got tough with me. They said, "Dad, don't lie to me anymore. I know what's going on." My marriage had crumbled, and I was the one who had wrecked it. That was a wake-up call. My daughter seemed stronger than I was in that moment, and that wasn't right. I committed to them that I would always tell the truth, and I did. I said you can ask me anything, and they did. Some of those conversations were tough, but my daughter had demanded more of me. They were being tough with me but not being hard on me—well, maybe some of the time they were. That was one of the best lessons they taught me. I wish I could take credit for this chapter, but I thank my daughter for this one.

Do you want to keep living the way you are? Is your way serving you? Is this who you are meant to be? If you are reading this book, likely the answer is no. Tell yourself enough is enough!

Get pissed off! If you don't get leverage on yourself, likely things will remain the same. As soon as you decide things are going to change, immediately fear sets in. That kind of fear is a good thing. Your mistaken identity, your false self, doesn't like change. But if you want to change your life, you're going to have to change.

■ MEDITATION ■

And as you wish that others would do to you, do so to them.

Luke 6:31 ESV

■ INSIGHTS ■

What did you learn from this chapter?

1.

2.

3.

■ ACTION ■

Enough is enough! Are you ready to get tough with yourself? This simple exercise could be exactly what you need. It's very empowering to take charge over your ego and your false self.

- List all the things in your life where it's time to say "I've had enough!"
- For each one, ask yourself, "Am I compromising myself?" Put a yes or no beside each one.
- Pick one thing you can do today to take charge of and to act on.

I want you to make a deal with yourself. Agree right now that you're going to demand more of yourself, be tough with yourself, but you're not going to be hard on yourself. You can't go wrong with this because you're going to *right* a *wrong*.

CHAPTER 13

Stop Should(ing) on Yourself!

You have been criticizing yourself for years and it hasn't worked. Try approving of yourself and see what happens.

—Louise Hay, author

You need to lighten up and smarten up.

We spend way too much time giving ourselves a hard time. We learned to do that, you know. When you were little, you weren't worried about what you should or shouldn't do until you were taught that you *should* be worried.

At a very early age, we started "should(ing)" on ourselves. The adults started it though! The adults—parents, teachers, people who judged us—told us what we *should* do. And you got used to being "should on" by others. So, you kept "should(ing)" on yourself.

Think about the things you tell yourself that you *should* do. You should work harder. You should get up earlier. You should stay later. You should eat better. You should get in better shape. You should be happier. That's the beginning of a very long list! Can you see all the judgment in that?

> **The adults—parents, teachers, people who judged us—told us what we *should* do.**

I spent a long time should(ing) on myself. I had made a lot of mistakes, and I'd hurt a lot of people, so I certainly had good reason to "should" on myself. I had lots of evidence and facts from my past that would back up why I *should* feel the way I did about myself and why I *shouldn't* be doing better. I spent years in therapy and counseling, dealing with the effects of a violent, abusive childhood, and my sins could be justified, so I had no reason to give myself such a hard time. But I still did despite how far I had come.

WHY ARE YOU STILL "SHOULD(ING)" ON YOURSELF?

The biggest source of shame and "should(ing)" on myself was my philandering and affairs. I was ashamed of my father, and I thought he was pathetic. Yet in some ways, I had become him, and I was doing things I shouldn't. I learned to "be a man" from my father. My dad used to bring women home with him. My dad would take me with him when he spent time with his girlfriends. That's what I learned. But that's not an excuse anymore.

I remember my dad used to keep his shotgun in the rafters of our basement. One time, he dragged my mom downstairs to the basement. He yelled at me to follow him. I was crying, my mom was fighting back, and I was scared. He grabbed his shotgun and stuck it down my mom's throat, and he said to me, "That's how you should handle a woman." Lucky for me though, I never adopted his abusive side.

I *should've* turned out a lot worse!

At a very early age, our intuitions pick up on the fact that something is "off." We look at the adults and watch how they act and what they say, and we can tell that something is off. We don't know their stories because they keep them secret, but we know something is off. You may still be should(ing) on your parents and on yourself, but try to understand they were should(ing) on themselves too and they didn't feel very good about themselves.

If they *should* on you, forgive them. They did the best they could. They could only do what they were able to do.

My father wasn't immune to the darkness and the violence he endured. He shouldn't have suffered but he did. My dad lost one brother in World War II; a second brother was wounded and shell-shocked and lived his life in the psychiatric unit of a veteran's hospital. My dad was wounded too and returned home and tried to find his way. It's no wonder men have really struggled. In the last hundred years we've seen a lot of war. When the men came back, they were wounded and found themselves struggling with who they were, where they fit in, and dealing with the aftershocks of violence and death.

Here's what I've learned. You should never measure anyone based on their past. You can never measure up to a list made up by others of what you should do or who you should be. You know what I've discovered after years of struggle? You don't have to struggle like I did.

There's only one thing you should do. You should stop being so hard on yourself and others.

▪ MEDITATION ▪

The Lord says, "I will teach you the way you should go;
I will instruct you and advise you."

Psalm 32:8 GNT

▪ INSIGHTS ▪

What did you learn from this chapter?

1.

2.

3.

■ ACTION ■

By now you see why you've been "should(ing)" on yourself.

- ■ What things do you tell yourself you *should* do? Which ones are true and good for you?
- ■ Who have you been "should(ing)" on? Make amends by admitting your judgment and open the door for their forgiveness.

We all need relief from judgment and criticism. Look at all the conflict created from some of the things you wrote down. You shouldn't be "should(ing)" on yourself. Think about that!

CHAPTER 14

Things Were Delicate

I can live for two months on a good compliment.

—Mark Twain

GOOD PEOPLE WILL HELP YOU ALONG THE WAY.

Growing up was hard! It was dark, violent, scary, and a little crazy. This book could be filled with stories from my memories that would shock you and that would still be haunting me if I let them.

School was hard too. I grew up in a low-income neighborhood. There was a mix of families at different levels, and down the street was social housing where a lot of the "bad kids" lived. I liked them though, and we were friends.

Early on I developed an inferiority complex, and I never felt good enough. I was sensitive. The kids at school teased me and bullied me. My parents couldn't do much for me because, in my eyes, they were damaged and crazy. So, I was left alone to find my way.

Like most kids I struggled to be liked. I didn't like the way kids treated me, but I wanted to be liked and accepted. Never quite feeling up to others' standards and not having a "normal life" at home, I set a bar for myself to be better, and I would spend most of my life striving to reach it yet never measuring up to it.

IT'S PROBABLY BEEN HARD FOR YOU TOO.

I struggled like most young people do, but for me, there were always people who supported me in a delicate way. They were teachers. Teachers who protected me, encouraged and supported me. They saw something in me that I couldn't see, and they nudged me, pushed me, and challenged me despite the delicate situation I was in.

There was Mr. Auld in grade five, who knew what was going on at home and did his best to protect me. In grade seven, it was Mr. Broome who pushed me in sports and strengthened my confidence. Mr. Hannah, my grade nine math teacher and basketball coach, demanded more of me. I can still hear him yelling at me in his raspy, gruff voice, "C'mon Dane'r, you're better than that." Mr. Feeney, my grade ten English teacher, showed me I had a talent, and I was bright, if I would just give myself a chance.

I quit high school three times, barely making it into grade ten, but here I am writing a book. How is that possible? It's possible because there have been people along my path who have encouraged, supported, and strengthened me. Most of those people never knew the impact they had.

> **There have been people along my path who have encouraged, supported, and strengthened me.**

My dad taught me things too. Despite his own struggles, he did his best to leave me with some lessons. When he was arrested when I was seven years old and charged with assault on my mom, he was ordered to quit drinking and start in A.A. He did quit and he never drank again. I think that helped me not become an alcoholic like him. It also taught me about commitment, although it would take years and other lessons for that to finally stick. He was a quiet man and didn't say much and couldn't do much for me. But me having to survive on my own only strengthened me. After his death, I found books he had been reading, like *The Power of Positive Thinking* by Dr. Norman Vincent Peale. That introduced me to books that would change my mind. I found his journals where he spelled out his remorse and asked God for forgiveness.

That helped me to forgive him. I found letters he had written home during the war. Although parts of the letters were redacted, I could feel his fear and pain. That allowed me to be more empathetic towards him and what he did, and I learned to be more sympathetic of others. When he died, he had arranged everything for us. He arranged his funeral, and he made a lot of arrangements for his boys to help lessen the struggle. Thank you, Dad!

Bob Proctor, my greatest teacher, became my mentor and a friend. Bob was a very special man. He saw the best in people, and he saw something in me. I could feel his belief in me, but I didn't believe in me. He never seemed to have a bad thing to say about anybody. He was the first person I met that didn't seem to judge anyone. He didn't judge me and that helped me to become free. He knew when to push me and he knew when to back off. But what he knew is what he could see in me, and I will forever be grateful for how he treated me and taught me to treat others.

You can be that for someone else. You can make a difference. You already have. Help people because you see the good in them. Plant seeds of good in their mind. Nurture them, protect them, talk to them. They are delicate too.

■ MEDITATION ■

He who did not spare his own Son but gave him up for us all, how will he not also with him graciously give us all things?

Romans 8:32 NIV

■ INSIGHTS ■

What did you learn from this chapter?

1.

2.

3.

■ ACTION ■

Whoever saw good in you, even if you didn't believe it, they were right about you. If they treated you well, it means they saw good in you. Accept it and thank them for it.

- Make a list of your angels in your life.
- Make a list of the gifts they saw in you.
- Write a note of thanks to one of the people who helped you believe in yourself when you didn't, even if you can't find them.

Consider the possibility that they were right about you. Some people were right about me. I just didn't believe them. They treated me with care, and they nurtured me. Perhaps you were worthy of the care that others offered you.

CHAPTER 15

Don't Make Stuff Up

It's sad that we never get trained to leave assumptions behind.

—Sebastian Thrun, entrepreneur, educator, and computer scientist

THE ENEMY IS A LIAR.

When I first began a relationship with God and started to study the Bible, I was introduced to the "enemy." In Christianity, he'd be called the devil. In psychology and personal development, it would be called ego or false self. I call it mistaken identity, and this cellmate (your ego) lies to you.

You've got to be careful what you make up in your mind through assumptions and your imagination. We tend to operate from a place of fear and insecurity. We've been taught to make assumptions. It's worth repeating here: the way you think is simply a habit you formed by what you learned from your parents and others, and we tend to make up worst-case scenarios.

> **The way you think is simply a habit you formed by what you learned from your parents and others.**

Most of us grew up watching our parents and the other adults in our life make stuff up about others. Without the facts, we view someone's actions, and we judge them and we make assumptions. Our imagination kicks in, and we make up all kinds of stories. Your mind is very powerful, and if you let it, it takes off in all kinds of directions. It's like a runaway train. One thought creates another and another and it becomes like a train of thoughts flashing before you while you're standing on the platform.

STOP THIS TRAIN. I NEED TO GET OFF.

It's like this: You get caught up in this moving picture in your mind. You don't like where it's going, you don't like what you're seeing, and you don't like what you're feeling. Sometimes it feels like it's out of control, but the only way to stop the train so you can get off is to stop thinking the way you're thinking. Literally you need to put the brakes on your thinking. If you're worried and you're making assumptions, you're likely letting your thoughts run away on you.

Assumptions create drama. Whatever you think about creates an emotional response, good or bad. That emotional response presents itself in your body in how you feel. People make assumptions, and they worry. That creates feelings of fear and doubt. That creates anxiety, and because they're afraid to express their emotions, they suppress their thoughts and feelings. This causes depression. *I didn't know that and* I created a lot of drama in my life. A lot of people are struggling with their mental health because of their assumptions.

I learned to make assumptions and second-guess myself because it was a survival tool. I had to guess and predict each move I made so I wouldn't get caught up in the violence. I had to bob and weave to avoid anger and fighting. In order to stay safe and avoid pain, I'd have to predict what my next move was. Later in life, I made a lot of assumptions about a lot of things, which got me into trouble. I can think of so many times when I would make things up in my mind. I'd get all worked up and stirred up, and my imagination would run away. If I kept a scorecard, I'd bet that 99 percent of the time I was off track, and I was wrong about what I was thinking and feeling, and that was creating my anxiety.

I'm so glad I figured that out. Now, if I'm worried and fearful, I'm responsible. I am consciously aware of what's going on and I can do something about it. I can stop the train and get off it. How about that? Wouldn't you like to take control of your own mental well-being? You can, you know! I know a lot of people who are struggling but don't need to if they understood what I'm trying to share with you in this chapter.

Remember, you are in control of what you think about, but you're the only one who can do anything about it. Nobody is going to do your thinking for you. I used to complain about things I was thinking and feeling, until I finally understood that I was the only one who could stop it. That's a hard pill to swallow at first because nobody can help you with that in the end. Someone can point the way like I am doing here but only you can take control.

Remember that when you're entertaining thoughts that don't feel good, it's because you're locked into a lie that you were told and believed, or you made stuff up in your mind that you now believe. The assumptions and lies never feel good.

We're so conditioned to question ourselves that, when we pick up a feeling that something or someone is off track, we assume there's something wrong with us, and we're on the wrong track. What keeps us stuck on the train? Why are we afraid to get off? We've been wrong so many times with our assumptions and we get to a point where we don't know if we can trust ourselves and our intuition. When your mind has been racing out of control you don't feel in control. And you don't trust yourself to make the right decision. When you're racing out of control you just hold on and you don't know what to do.

> ## When your mind has been racing out of control you don't feel in control.

Your intuition can help you determine what is true and what isn't. If something doesn't feel good, don't assume there's something wrong with you. It's likely that your intuition is on track, and it's picking up that there's something wrong with the situation. Don't make assumptions. Think, speak up, ask questions, don't assume.

You've got to take control of your mind and start to retrain it. The enemy wants to distract you from the truth. Your false self likes to punish you and make you feel lousy about yourself.

■ MEDITATION ■

And now, dear brothers and sisters, one final thing.
Fix your thoughts on what is true, and honorable,
and right, and pure, and lovely, and admirable. Think
about things that are excellent and worthy of praise.

Philippians 4:8 NLT

■ INSIGHTS ■

What did you learn from this chapter?

1.

2.

3.

■ ACTION ■

You've got to take an honest look at your assumptions. Are you willing to be honest with yourself and admit you're making assumptions?

- What seems "off track" in your life? What's going wrong?
- What assumptions are you making that keep driving the runaway train?
- What do you need to ask to find out if you're on the right track or off track?

The key to stopping making assumptions is to ask questions. Who do you need to address so you can clear up the drama you are creating?

CHAPTER 16

I'm Going to Be a Father!

Any fool can have a child. That doesn't make you a father. It's the courage to raise a child that makes you a father.

—Barack Obama, forty-fourth president of the United States

YOUR FATHER HAS A PLAN FOR YOU.

My daughter's mom and I were on and off again when we were dating because I didn't feel I was good enough, ready enough, and I was scared I would mess things up like all the other times in my past. There were so many things I didn't think that I was good enough for, including being a father. I assumed I would be bad at it, or worse, I would become an alcoholic and an abuser like my father.

As I navigated through my relationships, if I felt loved, I'd slowly, cautiously, share the stories of my past and the mistakes I had made. I was testing people to see if they would run away or accept me for who I was. I didn't accept or love myself, so how could they? Nonetheless, there was a deep-down feeling in me that I was a good man, so I pressed on. I've always been committed to becoming better. I've since learned to forgive my mistakes, and as I was making them, guilt-ridden and full of shame, I would push on to do better and be better.

People always ask me how I was able to make it through the pain of a horrific past, accomplish what I have, and become the person I am now. My answer is that I think the essence of who I am and always have been is integrity and God in me. He must have had a plan all along, because one day He spoke to me.

I remember it clearly. I was visiting a friend at her campground. Wendy was a friend from work, and I felt safe around her and her family. I knew I could trust her because she saw in me what I already felt was good in me; I just didn't believe it yet.

We walked and talked as her boys headed to the lake to swim and play. I remember watching them and thinking of summer nights with my father at Kiwanis Park Lake. My dad did his best to care for his boys, and I have fond memories despite his mistakes and brokenness as my father.

Wendy and I started to head back to her campsite with her young boys in tow. It was a clear, warm, sunny May afternoon, and something stopped me. I paused, looked up to the sky, and then turned to look back on Wendy's young sons walking and skipping with joy and happiness in their hearts.

> **I think the essence of who I am and always have been, is integrity and God in me.**

I felt a pull to look up to the sky again, and that's when the message came: "Doug, you're going to be a father!" I felt a rush of chills run down my spine as the message permeated my heart and soul. I knew it was a message from God. I knew it was the start of my life. I knew my daughter was being delivered to me.

I think He picked me at that moment because my struggles and story were meant for way more than what I felt I was worth. Self-loathing and shame were being replaced by forgiveness, love, hope, and a gift.

It was at that moment I felt I was ready to be a father. I returned home, excited to share my breakthrough, when my girlfriend, Eden's mom, announced she was pregnant and scared. I could hardly believe it. This couldn't have been a coincidence. The pregnancy wasn't planned, but when she told me, there was a calm and a strength that came over me. I said, "It's going to be okay. This is going to be great." I knew this was right on time.

My mistaken identity had me convinced that I wasn't worthy. I would come to learn and accept that I was created in the image of God, and He doesn't create any design flaws. I was going to be a father, and He would create my soon-to-be daughter in His image too, and they would be perfect.

I didn't have a relationship with God yet, but I'd meet Him from time to time as I went forward. I didn't believe in God, but I wanted to. I had friends that would talk about their faith and beliefs, but I felt very uncomfortable around those conversations. Even though I believed the messages I was getting came from God, in the moment I questioned them as I went forward. That doubt would carry on.

The day Eden was born, God spoke to me again. I felt like He wanted to be there and stand beside me. Eden's mom had been in labor for over twenty-four hours, and then suddenly Eden and their mom were at risk. We were rushed down the hall to emergency surgery, and in the confusion of it all, I got left behind, outside the operating room.

At the end of the hall, the sun was shining through the large windowpane, and I moved toward it as if I was being drawn to the light. I felt a strong presence as the warmth of the sun beamed through the glass and

I waited. Something was pulling on me. I looked up to the sun and whispered, "I feel you. You're here with me. I can hear You. Thank You for being here, God." And then Eden was born. I heard her cry for the first time, and I wept with joy.

Maybe it's time you discover the image that God has of you?

■ MEDITATION ■

"For I know the plans I have for you," declares the
LORD, "plans to prosper you and not to harm you,
plans to give you hope and a future."

Jeremiah 29:11 NIV

■ INSIGHTS ■

What did you learn from this chapter?

1.

2.

3.

■ ACTION ■

Allow the image of perfection to come through you. Give yourself a chance to see yourself the way God sees you. And allow others to see the good in you.

- Write a letter from God to you. Let God tell you all the beautiful, wonderful things He sees in you.
- Now, write a letter to yourself. Apologize to yourself and reassure yourself that the broken person inside is okay.

I don't care what you've done in the past or how you've been treated or how you treated yourself. It's time to see yourself in God's image and allow forgiveness for how you've felt about yourself.

CHAPTER 17

Meeting God

Whoever loves to meet God,
God loves to meet him.

—Muhammad, founder of Islam

IF YOU THINK SOMETHING'S MISSING IN YOUR LIFE, MAYBE IT'S GOD.

Don't get uncomfortable with the title of this chapter. Some people might. I used to get uncomfortable with the subject of God when anyone brought it up. If people asked me if I believed in God, I would say, "I'm spiritual." But I wasn't spiritual. I was ignorant. I didn't know God or much about Him.

I remember my first meeting with God. Clients of mine had asked me if they could teach a guided meditation at one of my workshops. One of the people working for me at the time had gone through it, and they loved it and suggested it would be a great addition to the workshop. I wouldn't say yes without knowing more about it, so I agreed to try it.

We met on a beautiful July day in a park near where I lived. We sat down at a picnic table together, and the two ladies explained what they were going to do. They asked me to close my eyes and relax, and they started to guide me through the meditation. They checked in with me to see if I was starting to connect to my "higher self." "How the heck would I know?" I blurted out. Knowing I felt uncomfortable, they told me to stare at a particular point on the picnic table.

The next thing I knew it was over. Yet in my mind I had traveled somewhere and seen something. They asked, "Can you tell us what you saw?" I said, "No!" I could have told them, but I was unwilling to speak about it. So, they asked me if I could write it down.

"What did you see?" they asked. I wrote the message that I received and passed it over while tears streamed down my face. What I wrote was the message I got from God.

In my guided meditation, I was on a beach, and God was a figure walking toward me. The scene I was in was a scene from the movie *Contact*, with Jodie Foster. To me, the movie is about the debate of belief in God versus science. I don't want to spoil the climactic scene, but Jodie Foster's character lands on an alien planet, and she sees a sinewy figure approaching her on the beach. It appears it's an alien who shows up as her deceased father. When they meet, she asks her father a question. In my meditation, her father represented God, and I'm in that scene. When God approaches me on the beach, His message to me is, "Doug, I'm going to hand you the keys to change the world with your voice and your words."

That was the first time I met God. It took me quite a while before I could tell this story to anyone because I worried people would think I'm nuts. The message was so clear, the vision felt so real, that I really believed I had met God, and He *was* talking to me.

I finally accepted the idea that I had met God and that He spoke to me. I've always felt like something was missing in me, and I've been searching for it. What was missing was God. He is in me and with me, and when I discovered that, a peace and release came over me. That was another moment of growth and awareness.

> **The message was so clear, the vision felt so real, that I really believed I had met God.**

I often ask people, "How's your relationship with God?" I can guess their answer based on how quickly they respond. Why don't more people believe in God?

I think it's because they are either ignorant (lacking awareness) like me, or they are hurt, angry, or lost. I was all of these.

You don't have to believe in God. You can believe whatever you want. But *I* believe, and if you ever feel something's missing in you, it might be the same thing that was missing in me.

■ MEDITATION ■

I love those who love me, and those who seek me diligently find me.

Proverbs 8:17 ESV

■ INSIGHTS ■

What did you learn from this chapter?

1.

2.

3.

▪ ACTION ▪

Consider the idea that God has been speaking to you. Open your mind to the possibility. If it was possible, consider the following questions.

- Have you ever felt God was talking to you? What did He say?
- If you asked Him what your purpose is, what would He tell you?
- Are you prepared to follow His direction?

The message I got felt so real, and it scared me at the same time. It felt true though. I want you to consider that the good you've heard about yourself from others is true, and that it is God talking to you through them.

CHAPTER 18

The Note

Don't doubt you are who I say you are.

I WAS SITTING IN a small coffee shop near my home with a close friend. I was going through another difficult time in my life (of my own making). Meghan was someone I could turn to for guidance and a listening ear. I sometimes think she's a real live angel on earth. She has a strong intuition and is closely connected to "*Spirit*". She has a *knowing* about her.

As we were chatting, out of the blue a middle-aged woman approached our table. "Excuse me," she said, seeming somewhat reluctant. "I don't mean to interrupt, but I was standing over there ordering my coffee, and God told me to write you this message."

I looked at her with curiosity. There was something warm and friendly about her. She passed me the note, and was gone as quickly as she had appeared at our table. The note was handwritten in pencil on the back of paper ripped from a nondescript notepad. I read the note and began to weep.

Here is the note:

I feel like I hear the Lord saying I have called you by name. Don't worry I have laid out a path before you and will give you the strength - everything you need to walk it Don't doubt you are who I say you are You do hear my voice and you are doing exactly what I called you to My love is a river flowing out of you You are a blessing to many I will supply all you need You have many stories to tell I will tell them through you DON'T DOUBT DON'T WORRY I am

I passed it to Meghan. She read it and asked me, "What do you think?"

I SAID, "I THINK IT'S A NOTE FROM GOD."

As I reread it, the words rang in my heart, chills went through me, and tears streamed again. The words in the note were almost word for word what I had been praying to God about since I met Him on the beach in my guided meditation. They were almost the exact words I had been speaking to God. "I do hear Your voice! I have stories to tell; help me tell them."

Later, I showed the note to another friend, who has a strong faith and relationship with God. After reading it, she said, "Amazing! You got a letter from God. I've never gotten one, and I believe in God deeply. You got a letter from God, Doug. Wow!"

That day in the coffee shop was one of many moments where God spoke to me. Each moment seemed real to me, but I had a hard time believing each one could be.

> **I'm not religious, but I do have a wonderful, blossoming relationship with God.**

I always felt something was missing. I thought it was what I had missed in my childhood because of the trauma and sexual abuse. I thought I had missed growing up with a mom in my life. I thought I missed what all children need when they're young. I thought I had missed my birth siblings in my life because I was adopted. I thought I was missing love from others. I felt there was a lot missing in my life, and it was all my fault.

The missing piece my whole life was a relationship with God. I was missing Him in my life, but I didn't realize He was *in* me the whole time, and He has been *with* me the whole time.

I'm not religious, but I do have a wonderful, blossoming relationship with God. You should meet Him; you'd love Him! As He loves you!

When I got the note, that was the beginning of the letting go and forgiveness I experienced. I read the note almost every day to remind me that God is with me. Some days I feel like God is talking to me, and other days, I question Him and wonder if He really sent that message.

Just today, as I was spending time with Him, I heard these words: *Who am I to question God and who He created? Who am I to question the good others see in me? Who am I not to accept who I am?*

■ MEDITATION ■

The thief comes only to steal and kill and destroy; I (Jesus) have come that they (you) may have life, and have it to the full.

John 10:10 NIV

■ INSIGHTS ■

What did you learn from this chapter?

1.

2.

3.

■ ACTION ■

It's the gifts we receive from others that make us feel whole
and that we matter. You matter and for others, they matter.
Make someone feel good about themselves today.

- Write them a short note and tell them what you see
  in them or what you think God would say to them
  about them.

CHAPTER 19

Why Don't You Love Me?

*Love yourself first and
everything else falls into line.*

—Lucille Ball, actress and comedian

No one can make you feel loved if you don't
first love yourself.

My third marriage was over, and I was stuck again.
Each time I failed in a relationship, someone would tell
me, "You have to love yourself first before you can love
or be loved."

What a crock, I thought. I didn't understand what
that really meant. I mean, I understood it intellectu-
ally, but I didn't relate to it on an emotional level. I

learned later in life that I had become disconnected from loving myself. It's no wonder I couldn't love myself because I believed I wasn't worth loving.

The idea that I needed to love myself became stronger, and it seemed like maybe that's what I was missing. But how does a person love himself? It seemed unreachable for me.

> **Like most keys to a better future, the secret lay unlocked in my past.**

I was sitting in my psychologist's office trying to figure out what was wrong with me, *again*. Like most of my revelations in my growth, the answer to self-love was wrapped up in a different perspective. That different perspective came from John, my psychologist. I enjoyed our talks and how he was able to get me to see the truth.

The answer was simple and elegant, and I didn't have to struggle. Like most keys to a better future, the secret lay unlocked in my past. You don't have to spend years uncovering the past, because that only causes you to focus too much on your mistakes and failures; it's like driving forward while looking in the rearview mirror. But a brief look behind you is okay so you can get a clearer picture and check your blind spots.

John asked me a couple of simple questions. He said, "If you could imagine you were that six-month-old baby that your birth mom gave up, and she was handing you over to someone else for adoption, if you could speak, why do you think she gave you away, and what would you say to her?"

I told him that I'd say, "Why don't you love me, Mommy? Why are you giving me away? What's wrong with me?" As soon as the words came out of my mouth, there was the answer. I had carried those questions around my entire life. I formed opinions and judgments toward myself, and as I failed—operating from my mistaken identity of being unwanted, unloved, and unlovable—I made more assumptions, created judgment, and formed conclusions about my*self*.

The next question provided the breakthrough I was searching for. John asked, "As a grown man and a father yourself, why do you think she gave you away?" My answer was filled with compassion and objectivity. I said, "I don't blame her. Many women like her did that, and she probably believed that life would be better for me. I'm sure she loved me, but she didn't love herself."

When I pieced together her story, it's no wonder she gave me up. By the time I found her, I was forty, and she had had six different children with four different men. Her first child died at a young age, her second son would see her come and go in his life, and she gave her last four children away for adoption. It was her choice. It wasn't about me.

When I found her, she didn't want to meet me. When my other birth siblings approached her, she denied she had children. She kept telling others she didn't want any children. She covered that up her whole life and kept it hidden.

It's no wonder. When I obtained records from my adoption, there was a letter in her file. When she became pregnant with her fifth child (me), she was ashamed and scared. She had to go before the court and the same judge who had granted the previous adoption order for my birth sister. The file and letter reveal her shame. She had to write a letter to the court explaining why she wanted to give up another child to adoption. She didn't love herself, and she had to hide from the shame of another pregnancy. I don't blame her. Who am I to judge? If I ever do meet her, I'll give her a hug and say, "Mom, you're okay."

My opinion had been that my mom or others in my life didn't love me. The facts were quite different. That's the problem we create in our heads. We create opinions or judgments instead of looking at the facts.

WHY WOULD YOU LOVE ME?

In all my relationships, I would question silently, "Why would you love me?" I found myself walking on eggshells most of the time. The ones that I felt secure in were the ones where they loved me more and expressed it, but I didn't love them the same way. The ones where I really loved them and I believed they were "the one" scared me and challenged my insecurities. It turns out

I couldn't know who "the one" was because I didn't love myself or know myself.

I couldn't stand it. The feelings of uncertainty conjured up assumptions and created fear. I was constantly doubting myself and making up all kinds of things in my mind. My imagination would take over, and most of my days were filled with anxiety and overthinking. What a trap I was in. I was stuck. I thought I was in love, and I couldn't bear the idea of the relationship ending, but I didn't like myself in the relationships or the way I was operating either.

When you live with someone, it's hard to hide from them. I tried to hide, and I got good at it. But the more I hid, the more I was lying to myself about who I was and who I wasn't.

We shouldn't rely on relationships to form us or make us whole. They are great for growth because you can't hide your true self from someone who loves you. Love is a magnifying glass. It allows us to see ourselves more clearly.

If you put all the weight on someone else to love you and to make you happy, you're going to lose every time.

John asked, "What will you do if this relationship you're in now doesn't work out?" I said, "I'll put all my attention on my relationship with my daughter." "Why would you want to put that on them?" he asked.

What a wake-up call! I decided that I wasn't going to rely on *anyone* for my happiness or for love. I decided to find out who I was, and then I'd fall in love with myself. When I made that shift, it didn't take very long. It was my opinion that I needed someone to love me, but the fact was that I needed to love myself, rather than rely on the love of others.

Muster up the courage to love yourself. You cannot truly love another if you do not love yourself. If you must, walk away from a relationship if you're not treated well or if you don't treat yourself well. You may need to be alone to learn to love yourself rather than being in a relationship and asking, "Why don't you love me?"

> **You cannot truly love another if you do not love yourself.**

Relationships don't define us. It is us who defines them, and that definition is based on a relationship we have with ourselves.

When you love yourself and you love your life, that's when you'll meet the love of your life. The love of your life could be you. Now that would be a great love story!

■ MEDITATION ■

*"And you must love the L*ORD *your God with all your heart, all your soul, all your mind, and all your strength." The second is equally important: "Love your neighbor as yourself." No other commandment is greater than these.*

Mark 12:30–31 NLT

■ INSIGHTS ■

What did you learn from this chapter?

1.

2.

3.

■ ACTION ■

Chances are you believe some things that cause you doubts. Do you love yourself? Do you feel worthy of love?

- Where did you get the idea that you weren't worth loving or are lovable?
- As an adult, how do you see that now?
- What advice would you give someone who feels like you?

I'm sure you're worth loving. You were disappointed when you were little, but now, you're an adult, and you don't need the opinion or love of others to love yourself.

CHAPTER 20

Is That Really True?

Your assumptions are your windows on the world. Scrub them off every once in a while, or the light won't come in.

—Isaac Asimov, Russian-born American writer

YOU'RE GOING TO HEAR A LOT OF THINGS THAT JUST AREN'T TRUE. If you're not careful, you may end up believing them. Social media has created a paradigm where you can create a narrative, which, if enough people pay attention to, can become true. Smartphones aren't that smart. We have easy access to a lot of misinformation that could steer us in the wrong direction and create polarization. In other words, you might believe things you might not otherwise because a large enough group of people do.

I was fed a lot of lies, and I fueled them with my own insecurities and fears. I developed the habit of making things up in my head, and I gave up control of my thinking by letting my emotions control my thoughts.

It was 2016, and I was in the middle of what I called "My Eeyore Year." You know, Eeyore from *Winnie the Pooh*; he always seemed sad and forlorn. That was me.

During that year, I was struggling with grief and with letting go, and I felt sorry for myself. I was so self-conscious and worried about what others were thinking of me. I was depressed and anxious.

I would head into Starbucks each morning for my reading time. Each day, my friend Pete would be there in his usual spot. Everyone there knew Pete. He is a gentle giant. He is tall and sturdy and has a kind and gentle way about him that makes people feel at ease. He is a Christian man, and he always has a piece of scripture on the tip of his tongue, which he uses to make his point.

Each day, I'd sit down, and he'd ask me how I was. I would answer in an Eeyore tone: "I'm fine." Each day it seemed I was saying the same things over and over again. I noticed Pete always asked me a question. He'd interrupt me when I was talking and he'd ask, "Is that true?" I'd keep talking, letting my answers be dictated by my feelings, and I'd keep going.

He'd interrupt again and ask, "Is that *really* true, Doug?"

On this particular occasion, I stopped my rambling and said, "Pete, I notice you ask me that question all the time."

He smiled warmly, and I finally caught it. I was making up a lot of things in my mind that just weren't true. I was learning a big life lesson. How I feel *is* real; however, what I'm feeling is not always *true*.

IS THAT REALLY TRUE?

I started using that question a lot. When I was having a bad day and feeling lousy, I'd pay attention to what I was thinking about and making up. If I was overthinking, I'd catch myself and ask, "Doug, is that really true?" I would tell myself, "Stick to the facts."

> **The fact is, I don't control my future or what others think of me, but the fact is, I can control my thinking.**

Then I'd say, "The fact is . . ." and then I would remind myself what was really true. The fact is, I'm a good man. The fact is, I can help people with my experiences. The fact is, I'm a good father. The fact is I'm a good partner. The fact is, I don't control my future or what others think of me, but the fact is, I can control my thinking. And now I do more and more!

As I was finishing the final edits to this book, I had dinner with Pete one night. I confessed, "I'm afraid about publishing the book."

"Why are you afraid, Doug?" he asked.

"I'm afraid I'm wrong about what I feel I know." And then, on my own, I countered with, "I know what I know because it's worked for me and others." I admitted that I was afraid of being attacked by people because I don't have an education, and I don't have a degree behind my name. Although I have a strong degree of experience. I went on: "I'm afraid because I want to be a disruptor in the self-help industry and mental health space, but I'm worried that people will try to take me down."

Pete looked at me with a serious face and said, "Can I ask you a question?"

"Sure," I said.

He asked, "Is that *really* true, Doug?"

We both smiled, and I said, "No, I know I'm on the right track. I wouldn't have been able to write this book without having developed the awareness and wisdom that comes from life's experiences and suffering, and nobody can argue with that."

So, here I am, publishing my first book of many to come. An educator once told me I'm a cognitive authority and I have direct experience and awareness to teach from and share. Now that's really true. I'll go with that and not worry about what others think of what I say in this book.

■ MEDITATION ■

And you will know the truth, and the truth will set you free.

John 8:32 NLT

■ INSIGHTS ■

What did you learn from this chapter?

1.

2.

3.

■ ACTION ■

Beware of what you see and hear, and ask yourself, "Is that really true? Do I accept this idea, or do I reject it?"

Think of things you've been embroiled in and dwelling on. Complete these sentences.

- Lately, I've been thinking that . . .
- But the truth is . . .

Stick to the facts, and train yourself so you're not making up things that aren't really true.

CHAPTER 21

The Elephant in the Room

There are no conditions to which a man may not become accustomed, particularly if he sees that they are accepted by those about him.

—Leo Tolstoy, Russian writer

YOU HAVE THE POWER TO TAME YOUR EMOTIONS.

Pete, whom I mentioned in the last chapter, asked one day, "Doug, have you ever heard the story of how your emotions are like an elephant?" I looked at him strangely wondering what was coming next.

He explained that emotions are like an elephant. Left untamed, an elephant can run wild, do all kinds of damage, and really hurt someone. That same elephant can be skillfully tamed. A thoughtful rider learns to partner with and direct the elephant so that good work can be done.

Pete said to me, "Do you want your emotions to cause you to be out of control and trample everything in your way and cause damage, or do you want to tame your emotions? You can be powerful and strong, but be in control of your emotions, rather than them controlling you."

Right then, I decided I was going to take control of my emotions. I decided to follow the instructions my mentor gave me, and that was to operate with emotional neutrality. So instead of reacting to things on autopilot, I decided to use intellectual objectivity.

> **You can be powerful and strong, but be in control of your emotions.**

How did I start to do that exactly? I started to use my intellect and *think* objectively about the things I was telling myself. I decided I would be neutral in my reactions, not allowing emotions to run wild. I started a simple habit of snapping my fingers and saying, "Nope, I'm not letting my emotions run my thinking." Our thinking is habitual, and so I started to create a new habit. It wasn't that hard, and it didn't take very long, but I had to pay attention to what I was thinking, feeling, and telling myself. I still do.

For a while, there were times when the elephant would get away from me. But quickly I would bring my emotions under control. I began to discipline myself by giving myself a command and following it. "Nope, I'm not letting my emotions run my thinking." And I would snap my fingers again.

When I mentor people and tell them this story, their first response is, "Do you mean I shouldn't care about anything or have any feelings?" That's not what I mean. I'm a very sensitive man with a huge heart, but I don't let my emotions control me. I cry at commercials and movies and love feeling my emotions, but I don't let them make stuff up and make me think things that aren't really true.

YOUR EMOTIONS MIGHT BE CONTROLLING YOUR THINKING.

Whether you like it or not or agree with me, you do have control over what you think about and you can learn to control your emotions and your thinking. But whether you exercise that control is another question.

Many people struggle with anxiety and depression, and they allow their emotions to control their thinking. I'm convinced now that most people don't have to struggle like they do if they understood how their mind works and how their thinking creates their reality.

Social media and our social support systems have created a narrative and brought so much attention to depression and mental health, that people easily get hooked into the story and start to wonder if they need to be diagnosed with something so that they can explain how they are feeling.

You can control your emotions with your thinking. Very few people understand that, and some of the people handing out diagnoses sure don't get that. It's a lot easier to remain a victim and blame your story or circumstances on how you're feeling and let the elephant trample all over you and your life. It's a lot easier to diagnose yourself in order to justify yourself, but it's a heck of a lot better and more empowering to take control of your thinking so you can tame the elephant and befriend it.

You can stay stuck, or you can put your stake in the ground, claim your personal power, and say, "I'm not letting my emotions rule my thinking!" You don't have to suffer. Don't live your life as an untamed elephant.

If you want to tame your emotions, you have to take control of your thinking, and that means you're going to have to stop doing certain things. I'll explore with you more what those things are and how you can begin to practice this in the next chapters.

■ MEDITATION ■

A person without self-control is like a city with broken-down walls.

Proverbs 25:28 NLT

■ INSIGHTS ■

What did you learn from this chapter?

1.

2.

3.

▪ ACTION ▪

When you catch yourself letting your emotions drive your thoughts, snap your fingers and say, "Nope, I'm not letting my emotions run my thinking."

- Make a list of the things where your emotions are causing damage.
- What situations in your life feel like they are out of control?
- If you could tame these situations, what could you do differently?

You've been given the gift of your mind and your intellect. Train them. Use them wisely. You can keep giving up control or you can take control of your life. What's it going to be?

CHAPTER 22

Single Dad, Poor Dad

Instead of feeling sorry for yourself, do something about it.

—Eminem, American rapper and record producer

BEING POOR IS NOT A GREAT WAY TO LIVE.

I started out poor when I was young. I figured out how to succeed in life financially, but I was still poor. Poor me! I felt sorry for myself. I had a great story to use as an alibi and to stay stuck as a victim.

I remember my first Christmas as a single dad. I've had a tradition on Christmas Eve where I would go shopping to buy myself a gift, and then I would go for lunch.

After leaving my marriage, the first Christmas Eve was the only day I would be able to see my daughter over the holidays. We spent the morning shopping, and then I dropped them off early in the afternoon. As they left my car and headed into my former family home, tears streamed down my face. *Poor me*, I thought. *You're such a piece of crap, Doug. You're a loser. Who are you to profess you can help others when you've wrecked your marriage and lost your daughter?*

Pulling out of the driveway, I felt lost. I had nowhere to go. I didn't want to go home, so I went for a late lunch at my favorite restaurant. The staff there know me, and they are always friendly. That would be a safe place to go. Ashamed and embarrassed and all by myself, I sat down at the bar, feeling sorry for myself.

I didn't notice at first but a few minutes later I saw that I was the only one left in the restaurant. Here I was sitting alone on Christmas Eve all by myself in an empty restaurant. *Poor me*, I thought again.

DON'T LET THAT ELEPHANT IN.

Later that winter I was in a restaurant, and I saw a father with his two kids. I could tell he was a single dad, and he looked sad and lost. I started to see myself in other fathers. There was this lonely look about us. Our shoulders drooped and we couldn't make eye contact. I'm sure that we all felt embarrassed and ashamed that we were single dads—poor dads.

There's nothing worse than feeling poor and feeling like a victim. I had lived with shame my whole life. It would come and go during my highs and lows, and finally I got fed up with it.

I became inspired to help others because we shouldn't live our lives with guilt and shame. We were taught that it's weak if we show our emotions. We are taught that we must be strong. If we reveal our vulnerability, we run the risk of losing the ones we love. How could they love a man who is *weak*?

> **Through accepting forgiveness from the One who has forgiven us, I was able to move on.**

My memory goes back to my poor dad. Later in my dad's life, after all his mistakes, he spent his days in his La-Z-Boy chair, racked with arthritis, watching television, reading books, and eating TV dinners, trying to find forgiveness, feeling sorry for himself. Poor him.

It's no wonder I grew up thinking and acting the way I did. So many mistakes, so many losses, and it was all that kind of thinking that made me *feel* so poor. But finally, through accepting forgiveness from the One who has forgiven us, I was able to move on. I made my mind up that I was going to be a good man and a good father. And so, I began to change how I thought about myself and my feelings began to change from poor to grateful.

It took some time to believe it and some more time for it to come true. But now, as I write this, I smile to myself and think of that single dad, that poor dad I once was.

Life is lighter, and I laugh at myself more now. When you're a victim you take yourself and life way too seriously. Life can be hard, but life is also simple. If you remain a victim, life is way too hard.

■ MEDITATION ■

Brothers, I do not consider that I have made it my own. But one thing I do: forgetting what lies behind and straining forward to what lies ahead.

Philippians 3:13 ESV

■ INSIGHTS ■

What did you learn from this chapter?

1.

2.

3.

▪ ACTION ▪

Self-pity is not limited to us men. I know you may be feeling sorry for yourself, and I empathize with you but that's not the way you want to live, is it?

- List all the ways you feel sorry for yourself and feel like, "Poor me!"
- Is that the way you want to see yourself? Is that who you really are?
- How can you think of yourself differently, in a way that is more empowering?

In the next chapters I'll help you stop getting stuck in your "poor me" attitude.

CHAPTER 23

Stop It

Change the way you look at things,
and the things you look at change.

—Wayne Dyer, self-help author
and motivational speaker

THE BEST WAY TO RID YOURSELF OF NEGATIVE THOUGHTS IS TO STOP THINKING THEM.

One day I was talking with my psychologist John, and he told me to "Stop it!" It was some of the best advice I've ever received, and I think it can help you too. I was sitting in John's office, and the habit of second-guessing myself, overthinking, ruminating on my problems, and worrying about my future continued to breed my anxiety and fears.

I was describing a situation and how I was feeling when John interrupted me. It wasn't the first time I had talked about the situation with him. He leaned in and said, "I've got a suggestion for you." I leaned in eager to hear his advice. He said, "Doug, you no longer need to come see me anymore. If you follow this strategy, it will be a game changer for you.

> **Whenever you think of something that you don't want to, or whenever your second-guessing starts, you just stop thinking about it.**

"What is it?" I asked. I was all ears, hoping for a solution.

"It's called thought-stopping," John said. I was earnest to hear more. He explained that it works like this: whenever you think of something that you don't want to, or whenever your second-guessing starts, you just stop thinking about it. He smiled at me and sat back in his chair, waiting for my response.

"That's it?" I asked, surprised. There had to be more. It couldn't be that simple. John explained that everything I teach when mentoring clients is all about the strength of the mind and controlling what you think. He was right. And I wasn't following that.

So, I began to train my mind. I formed the habit of thought-stopping. And then I thought that it couldn't be this simple. *This'll never work*, I thought, but it did.

Taking control of your thinking and not letting what's going on in your life control your thinking is hard work, at first.

You can't just stop thinking about what you're thinking about, right? Wrong!

When it gets hard, it's easy to think it must be difficult. Thinking is the hardest work you'll do, but if you train your mind and build up your mental muscles, you get really strong, really fast, and it gets easier.

STOP IT!

When you're thinking about something that makes you feel uncomfortable, fearful, or anxious, just *stop it*. As a father and a mentor to others, I often say, "Stop it." If you continue on that train of thought, you'll get off track.

> **Don't play the victim and give up your personal power to others.**

You might think that's easy to say but not as easy to do. You're right, but don't play the victim and give up your personal power to others and allow the influence of friends, family, or circumstances to rule your thinking. Stop it!

■ MEDITATION ■

So don't worry about tomorrow, for tomorrow will bring its own worries. Today's trouble is enough for today.

Matthew 6:34 NLT

■ INSIGHTS ■

What did you learn from this chapter?

1.

2.

3.

■ ACTION ■

Are you prepared to stop it? If you don't, you'll stay stuck in your thinking and stuck in your life.

- What are some negative things you keep thinking about that you need to say "Stop it"?
- Make a short list, read each item out loud, and then say, *stop it*. Do this every day for a week.

Make your mind up that you're no longer going to be a victim of circumstance or a victim of any kind. Stop thinking about things that aren't true or that belong in your past.

CHAPTER 24

Grow Up

No one is born hating another person because of the color of his skin, or his background, or his religion. People must learn to hate, and if they can learn to hate, they can be taught to love, for love comes more naturally to the human heart than its opposite.

—Nelson Mandela

YOU CAN'T "GROW UP" UNTIL YOU LEARN TO CARE FOR YOUR INNER CHILD.

Sometimes I still have emotional responses to situations that cause the "broken little boy" in me to act out. I remember my mom yelling at me whenever I was upset: "Why don't you grow up?" What a dumb question for a young boy. How do you even do that? Would she even have an answer for that? If she did, it probably wouldn't make sense to me.

The times when I needed my parents the most, I would be met with these statements: Grow up! What's wrong with you? Why are you crying? I had a lot of questions running through my mind as I was growing up, which continued to fuel the question: "What's wrong with me?"

> **Memories, experiences, hurts, and cutting words are deeply embedded, and they often hijack our reactions.**

Many of us were told to grow up. That was a childish response from chidlish adults who were raising us. They didn't know any better, and most of them were just doing their best with what they had.

When I was being raised in the late sixties and early seventies, parents didn't have the resources we have today and the knowledge that's been garnered through parenting psychology. Today, there is no reason why any parent cannot grow up and parent their children from an adult perspective. I often think you should be required to take a test before you can parent.

Our emotional subconscious mind is a powerful thing. Memories, experiences, hurts, and cutting words are deeply embedded, and they often hijack our reactions when they are triggered by situations and other people. I was acting like a child.

My first counselor, Ellyn, taught me to parent the little boy in me. She asked me, "What would you say to young Doug as he was going through that mess and witnessing the violence? What would you say to him when he was feeling ashamed and guilty?" These were feelings I took on from the abuse. But just because they are learned, doesn't mean they have to be part of the way I operate now.

When I start to feel childlike emotions, I check myself and I remind myself that everything is okay and I'm okay. Then I parent my young self from my adult self. If I act out, I admit it and share it with those who love me. And I'm forgiven.

Another parent figure in my life, Rita, had suggested to me that each night before I go to sleep, I talk to the little boy in me to calm his fears and tell him he's okay. I would lay down in bed and under my breath I would whisper, "You're okay, Doug. You're a good boy. None of the darkness was your fault. You're not responsible. You're a good boy. You're a beautiful young boy, Doug, and I love you." At first, I would cry because I felt sorry for that little boy. I wasn't feeling sorry for myself; I felt sorry for my former self.

THAT WORKED A LOT BETTER THAN TELLING MYSELF TO GROW UP.

Anger, jealousy, resentment, futility, judgment, hate, frustration, and anxiety are all childlike emotions and are learned responses. They are human responses. Our parents judged us, and they judged themselves after making childlike parenting mistakes. Telling us to grow up was not the answer we needed, and it just bred more judgment. We need to let go of judgment by growing up ourselves.

> **It's time that you take back your personal power and shed your mistaken identity that convinces you that you're weak and powerless.**

I used to act like a child. I'd stomp and cry and whine that *you don't understand me.* I used to feel sorry for myself and generate sympathy from others. It was a great defense mechanism to avoid being myself and disconnecting from myself and others. It worked really well because I could play the blame game. I got good at blaming others because they didn't understand me. Besides how could they sympathize with me because they didn't go through what I went through? What a pathetic way to live.

It's okay to have a childlike response and become aware of the cause, but it's not okay to keep playing the victim and acting like a child. It's time that you take back your personal power and shed your mistaken identity that convinces you that you're weak and powerless. You're not weak. Just because you have weaknesses does not make you a weak person.

Some people are aware of their childhood wounds, but they still act like a hurt little child. I did. We even invented a term for it—"Adult Child Syndrome." Others are unaware, and they continue to act out and never grow up. Then they get into relationships, and they raise children who act out.

Usually this is where it shows up the most. If you act like a child, it's hard to hide. If you try to hide, you become disconnected and distant, and the questions begin. And then you question yourself, and your partner questions themselves.

When you begin to take care of your inner child, you will develop the maturity you need to raise healthy children of your own. At the very least you'll grow up and stop acting out. Acting like a child breeds more shame.

I found a way to grow up. I decided I would take a positive view on what happened to me. I decided that it was good that I landed in that family, and what I endured was good. My suffering gave me a perspective that could help others who are still struggling. Now, that's a grown-up viewpoint.

■ MEDITATION ■

And the child grew and became strong, filled with wisdom. And the favor of God was upon him.

Luke 2:40 ESV

■ INSIGHTS ■

What did you learn from this chapter?

1.

2.

3.

■ ACTION ■

Grow up right now. It doesn't have to take you a lifetime. It can be instant if you're willing to look at this differently. Are you?

- Think of a situation where the young person in you was reacting with childlike emotions.
- If your child came to you for help, as an adult, what advice would you give them?
- What does your inner child need to hear from you now that you're an adult?

Okay, now that you've done the exercise, what are you going to do next? Will you change your perspective on your childhood?

CHAPTER 25

Sweaty Palms, Big Heart

Just when the caterpillar thought the world was over, it became a butterfly.

—Chuang Tzu

ANXIETY COMES FROM THINKING ABOUT YOURSELF TOO MUCH.

My palms still sweat when I'm nervous or when I start worrying about what others think of me. I remember when I was young, how nervous I would get around others. I just wanted people to like me and accept me. I had such a negative attitude toward myself because of who I thought I was or wasn't. When I think about it, I was a beggar. I was begging for the approval of others, and that's a losing game. No wonder I'd sweat.

I wanted kids at school to like me. I went to school with the so-called rich kids, and I hung out with the poor kids on my block. The rich kids teased me because I was poor, and the poor kids teased me because they were teased too. I didn't like the rich kids because they teased me, yet I wanted to be liked by them. Imagine trying to become someone you loathed, and you loathed yourself. Imagine the inner conflict that sets up.

My palms have been sweating for a long time and I kept thinking there must be something wrong with me. When I'd meet people, I would have to wipe my hands on my pants before I shook their hands. I remember one time I was in a Catholic church service, and the part where you greet people and shake hands was coming. I got so nervous leading up to it. My hands were sweating, and I was worried what the person would think when they felt my cold, clammy hands.

My sweaty palms came from my experiences and how I saw myself. When I'm alone or with people I trust completely, I'm relaxed and calm, and my hands are dry. My sweaty palms are a sign that I'm overthinking and worrying too much about myself or wondering if I'm okay.

My mentor once said, "Doug, you're self-centered." *No, I'm not*, I said to myself. I didn't even know what he meant. He explained that I spent too much time thinking about myself. He offered me something that caused an instant shift in my mind.

STOP THINKING ABOUT YOURSELF SO MUCH.

Underneath all the anxiety and depression I created because of my self-centeredness and extreme self-consciousness, I discovered I have a big heart. I've always cared deeply for people, and I've been very sensitive to others' feelings along with my own.

That knowing alone did not stop me from making mistakes and hurting others. I had set up an inner conflict in my heart. I believed I was a good person, but I wasn't always doing good things. As I struggled to get it right, I continued to criticize myself for my mistakes. I kept beating myself up, and at the same time, trying to build myself up.

> **I had set up an inner conflict in my heart.**

Finally, I was done beating myself up. I wasn't treating myself fairly. Others in my shoes with my story would have made mistakes too. I didn't deserve to be so hard on myself. If you treated me like I was treating myself, I wouldn't tolerate it.

I decided to turn my thoughts outward and focus on ways my big heart could help others. I simply decided to think about others and their well-being more. All there is, is love or fear, so I chose love. I figured if I poured my heart and love into others, that was a good idea. The more I did that, the more calm and serene I became.

I continue to work toward being equable. In other words, I practice relaxing my mind, focusing on the moment, and focusing on helping others. I don't react, and I'm very patient. That was a choice I made, and I continue to practice.

I love these parts of the "Serenity" chapter from James Allen's amazing little book, *As a Man Thinketh*.[1] This little book has contributed to my peace in so many ways. This is who I aspire to be!

> **I practice relaxing my mind, focusing on the moment, and focusing on helping others.**

"Calmness of mind is one of the beautiful jewels of wisdom," Allen writes. "It is the result of long and patient effort in self-control. Its presence is an indication of ripened experience, and of a more than ordinary knowledge of the laws and operations of thought. The calm man, having learned how to govern himself, knows how to adapt himself to others; and they, in turn, reverence his spiritual strength, and feel that

---

1. James Allen, *As a Man Thinketh*, (Summit, NJ: Start Publishing, 2013)

they can learn of him and rely upon him. The more tranquil a man becomes, the greater is his success, his influence, his power for good."

When people ask how I'm doing, my answer is, "I'm the best I've ever been in my life because I'm the furthest away I've ever been from the fear of criticism and judgment and self-centeredness. Each day I move farther away. And the farther away I get from that, the better I feel."

The faucet on my sweaty palms only drips when I'm worried about what others think of me.

I hope you will stop worrying about what others think of you. Use your mind properly, and don't waste the gift of it. Don't waste your time worrying about tomorrow. All you have is today. Follow your heart, and you'll be fine. I promise.

■ MEDITATION ■

Casting all your anxieties on him, because he cares for you.

1 Peter 5:7 ESV

■ INSIGHTS ■

What did you learn from this chapter?

1.

2.

3.

■ ACTION ■

Are you sweating the small stuff? Are you making the small stuff big and the big stuff bigger? You've got to stop focusing on yourself and what you think is wrong. Change your mind.

- Make a list of things that you worry about and what others think of you or what they will do.
- Strike out all the things your mind tells you, "You shouldn't be worrying about this."
- What's left? Can you do anything about it? If you can, do it. If not, let it go.

I'm sure you can find more positive things to focus on. Go help someone who needs it. Lift someone up from their despair. If you lie around worrying about yourself, it will be a lonely life. You're better than that, and you deserve better, but only you can claim it.

CHAPTER 26

Guilty Verdict

Guilt is the thief of life.

—Anthony Hopkins, actor, director, and producer

Nobody can condemn you after you've been set free.

Who determines whether your conduct is good or bad? In a court of law, you're innocent until proven guilty. Usually, the burden of proof is on the prosecution to prove your guilt. The prosecutor is the one who presses charges and tries to prove you're guilty.

Are you guilty? Are you still feeling like a victim? Who's the prosecutor in your life? You? Family, friends, coworkers, pop culture, society?

Like most of us, you've made mistakes, or you've hurt people, and you're still paying for it. You shouldn't still feel guilty long after you've served your time and paid the price. Stop paying for your mistakes over and over. If you keep looking backwards on the past with guilt or resentment, that's where you'll stay—in the past, locked in a prison.

> ## Stop paying for your mistakes over and over.

Guilt means you hold on to negative thoughts and emotions toward *yourself*, and resentment means you hold on to negative thoughts and emotions toward *someone else*. You keep making others feel guilty because of your resentment, which only feeds your own feelings of guilt.

Guilt is always associated with the past. You never feel guilty for something you haven't done. Feeling guilty is a waste of your time and energy. If you're going to do that you may as well stay locked up and throw away the key.

FREEDOM FROM YOUR PAST MEANS FORGETTING THE PAST.

Don't use your memory and imagination against you to dredge up the past. If you really want to let go of the guilt, you're going to have to forgive yourself and forget the past. Most people want to make you feel guilty because they feel guilty and think you should too.

People in your life who "make you feel guilty" live in the past. Just because they live there, it doesn't mean you have to. I know what you're thinking: It's not that easy.

For too long I would dredge up my past. I had a lot to feel guilty about, and I carried resentment around for too long. I was very resentful toward my mom and my dad. My mom continued to struggle with mental illness and alcoholism and my dad wasn't much of a father.

The only time I saw my mom was for visits to her lame apartment, wherever she was living at the time, for the obligatory birthday or holiday. As I'm writing this chapter, it's Thanksgiving weekend, and I'm thinking of the weekends I would head to my mom's for Thanksgiving dinners.

There wasn't much to be thankful for. The only thing I would be thankful for on those days was the end of the visit. By the time I'd arrive, my mom would be drunk and sloppy. Because of the shock treatments, her mouth and face would have this strange, contorted shape when she drank. The drunker she got, the worse her face and her slur got. I was resentful of her. Not because of what she had done to me, but more for what she was still doing to herself.

The dinner was burned; she was too drunk to keep an eye on the turkey, and so it was wrecked. She was wrecked, and my life felt wrecked too.

I felt guilty about how I felt about her. I felt guilty that I didn't want to see her. I felt guilty that I just wanted to leave. I had no reason to feel guilty, but we learn to feel guilt and make others feel guilty.

It was hard to forgive my mom, and I didn't— until I learned *how to* forgive. People always talk about forgiveness, but very few understand it. They can't explain it, and they can't show you how to forgive.

Forgiving my mom came in a moment when I didn't expect it. She was dying of lung cancer and spent the last couple of months of her life in a palliative care hospital. One day, near the end when she couldn't speak anymore, I told her the story about being abused. This was in the middle of me unblocking the memories and after I told her what had happened to me, she squeezed my hand with love as if to say, it's okay Doug. That's all I needed. It was a gift I wasn't expecting, and I was able to forgive her.

You can let go of your guilt.

For me, I went to the only true source of forgiveness and the only One I needed to go to. I learned to accept forgiveness and forgive myself and leave my guilt and resentment where it belongs, in the past.

A couple thousand years ago, there was a man who came here to tell us how to live, love, and forgive, but we didn't listen to Him, and we're still not listening. We're listening to everyone else, and we're still worried about what others think. Maybe it's time to listen.

Your sins are forgiven. You can let go of your guilt. You are free!

You can free yourself from your emotional prison and live a fulfilling life. Or you can remain a victim of your own making. It's your choice. It's simply a decision, but you're the only one that can make it.

I was stuck in an emotional prison that I had built. The key to my freedom lay inside me. I felt stuck most of my life, and I blamed circumstances and situations, others, and especially myself for my feelings of inadequacy. I had no idea that freedom was within my grasp the whole time.

When I finally started to win, it was because I adopted a new way of thinking, and I began to follow it. If you want to win in life, forget the past, forgive your mistakes, and stop feeling guilty.

You're free to go! That's what a judge says to you when you're innocent of a crime, you're wrongly accused, or your sentence is up.

■ MEDITATION ■

He himself bore our sins in his body on the tree, that we might die to sin and live to righteousness. By his wounds you have been healed.

1 Peter 2:24 ESV

■ INSIGHTS ■

What did you learn from this chapter?

1.

2.

3.

▪ ACTION ▪

Are you open to the idea of what this chapter says? Would you even consider that you could let go of guilt and resentment quickly and easily? That's your only problem. You learned to hold onto guilt and resentment, and you may not want to let it go. But if you do, you can free yourself and free others in your life. I have a few simple questions for you.

- Do you want to let go of your guilt—yes or no?
- Would you feel better if you did—yes or no?
- What's one thing you have felt guilty about for way too long?
- And what's something you feel resentful about toward someone, but it is a waste of time?

If you don't want to go back to prison, follow my plan.

1. Don't spend any time in the past. There's nothing back there that you need.
2. Accept the idea that the plan is simple, and you can be free.
3. Take responsibility for staying stuck in a prison of your own making and never go back.

CHAPTER
27

Let It Go!

*Sometimes letting things go is an act of
greater power than defending or hanging on.*

—Eckhart Tolle, spiritual teacher and author

Focusing on the past is a waste of energy.

Life can feel hard, but too often we make it harder
for ourselves. It doesn't mean that life won't put road-
blocks and challenges in our way, but it does mean we
can look at those any way we want.

Any energy you put toward negative things is a
waste of your time. Put your valuable energy toward
good. Imagine that each day you are given credits to
use. When the credits run out, you don't get any more
for the day. If you were given credits every day, and
each thought, word, feeling, or action was a credit, you
wouldn't waste them.

I've wasted too much of my life in worry, doubt, and fear. I had no idea that I was causing my own anxiety, depression, and *dis*ease by holding onto and reliving the past. It was a wake-up call when I realized it was *me* causing my pain. Recently, my mentor Bob Proctor passed, and I was asked to share how he had changed my life or what he had taught me. The greatest gift Bob gave me was the lesson of letting go. He left me in a good place, armed with the awareness that I could let go.

I struggled for a long time as a victim of my past, and I kept trying to figure out what was wrong with me and why I felt so lousy most of the time. I spent years thinking my healing was difficult and complicated and would take a long time. It was because that's what I believed. But when I met Bob, he suggested something to me that I wasn't willing or ready to accept. He asked, "What if it was easy, Doug? What if you could just let it go?"

There's no way something so difficult and so painful could be simple and easy to let go of. How could it be? I didn't believe anybody could understand what I had been through; therefore, they wouldn't understand how to let it go, not even Bob.

Bob would say, "Let it go, Doug." I remember telling him that things were different for me (or so I thought), and he didn't really understand me. I said, "You didn't come from where I did, and you didn't suffer the effects of trauma and abuse like I did." He looked at me with his wise smile and simply responded, "Hmm."

I was going to prove to him he was wrong, that it *isn't* simple and that there isn't a universal answer for everyone, no matter what their past circumstances were. Well, I was wrong. Each time I was feeling like I was stuck in the same place, his answer was the same: "Let it go, Doug."

I wasn't in the same place, but it felt that way. I was making progress, but it didn't feel like I was. If you looked at my life, it looked like it was getting better. And it was. But it didn't feel like it was. Finally, he said, "I can only help you if and when you can accept the idea that letting go *is* easy."

When I was attempting to let go, it wasn't easy because I was convinced it must be hard. Finally, I accepted that it *was* simple and it was; the answer was quite simply, letting go.

IF YOU WANT TO LET GO, FOLLOW THE RULES.

Nature, us included, operates by nature's laws. There are rules on how our minds work, which drive our brains and nervous systems, but I wasn't following the rules. After learning some simple rules, I was able to apply them, and quickly things started to change. I now know anyone can let go of their past and stop feeling like a victim. It's not hard, it's not difficult, and it doesn't take very long. Now I understand what Bob meant when he said, "It's so simple, yet it's so misunderstood."

If you follow these rules each day, you can live a beautiful, joy-filled life. Think of your life as a scale with two dishes. Imagine one side of the scale has a pile of little pebbles, which represent all your struggles and negative thoughts and feelings. Imagine you follow the rules, and each day you move one of the tiny stones to the other side of the scale. Soon the scale starts to tip in your favor, and soon the scale on the positive side weighs more. That would be a weight off your shoulders.

> **I now know anyone can let go of their past and stop feeling like a victim.**

Here are my rules I adopted for letting go.

One: Don't look back on your past. Don't talk about your past and don't think about your past. There's nothing back there that you need in order to go forward. If there is, trust your memory to bring it to the present as you go forward.

Dwelling on my past only brought up memories and that was not helping me go forward. In fact, it was keeping me stuck. Most people are taught to live that way.

Two: Don't worry about your future. You can't control it, and you might not have one if you waste your days thinking that you can.

The only reason you live in the past and worry about the future is, it's a habit you learned, and you can unlearn and relearn.

Three: Live one day at a time and focus your thinking on what you want, not on what you don't want.

I decided to live my life one day at a time. I decided to focus my thinking on what I wanted my future to look like and stop trying to control how it would happen.

Four: Everything is your responsibility. It wasn't your fault, but now it's your responsibility.

Everything that had happened to me, all the suffering from my past and all the mistakes, were my responsibility now. There's strength that comes from taking responsibility for your life. It seemed like there was an instant release. I was free; I was in control.

My hope is that you won't remain a victim and stay stuck in an emotional prison. It's just plain wrong that people stay stuck like I used to. Stop wasting your life. Change your mind, and change your thinking.

For me it's really simple now. Bob said, "If your way isn't working, why not try mine?" If you're still stuck and struggling, why not accept the idea that you can let it go? It's really that simple.

■ MEDITATION ■

*Can any one of you by worrying add a single hour to
your life?*

Matthew 6:27 NIV

■ INSIGHTS ■

What did you learn from this chapter?

1.

2.

3.

■ ACTION ■

You can see the theme of this book is about letting go. If you're holding on tight, that's a problem. You're holding onto the things that you can't control, or you're locked into the idea that you can't let go.

Can I ask you a question before you go on? Did this chapter make sense? If it did, are you willing to change your mind? If it didn't make sense, maybe you're not ready to let go. I wasn't, but I wasted too much time defending my mistaken beliefs. Be honest with yourself. You're the only one who can change your mind.

- ■ What do you need to let go of?
- ■ How long have you been carrying this around? Isn't it time to let it go?
- ■ If you did let it go, how would it help you?

How about you try letting go and see how you feel? It's not that hard, so don't make it hard.

One more thing you must let go of. You must let go of worrying about what people will think of you if you do let go. Don't worry about it; you'll fly!

CHAPTER 28

The Cure

Once you realize you deserve a bright future, letting go of your dark past is the best choice you will ever make.

—Roy T. Bennett, Zimbabwean politician

YOUR VERSION OF YOUR PAST DOES NOT DICTATE YOUR FUTURE.

I often think about how young people struggle and how they end up turning into adults who struggle like I did. I hope this chapter sheds some light on things for you. Like young people I have helped, I stayed stuck because I wasn't willing to change my perception on my story.

It took me way too long, and I made it hard when it didn't have to be. Our mental health care system seems to have it wrong for too many people. From my experience and what I've learned, I think we are going about the problem we face the wrong way. I believe most people don't need to struggle as they do or at least they could struggle a heck of a lot less if they changed their mind. People need to change their minds to believe that they can take control of their mental well-being. They need to change their mind about their past and they need to change their mind about the story they are telling themselves. The mental health care system needs to change the narrative around mental health, and it must change the way it's approaching it.

The cure is simple! You can learn how your mind works and how it controls your brain and nervous system. I remember when I finally began to understand this.

> **People need to change their minds to believe that they can take control of their mental well-being.**

I was reading the book *Psycho-Cybernetics*, by Maxwell Maltz. In the book, he explains what he calls your "Automatic Success Mechanism." He says you have a machine that you operate, and it's directed by the self-image, the image you hold of yourself. One of our biggest problems that causes us the most trouble is the opinion we hold of ourselves.

Here's what he wrote: "There is a widely accepted fallacy that rational, logical, conscious thinking has no power over unconscious processes and that to change negative beliefs, feelings or behavior, it is necessary to dig down and dredge up material from the 'unconscious.' It is *conscious thinking* which is the 'control knob' of your unconscious machine."[1]

So, part of the cure is to direct your thoughts and not let your thinking be directed by others. Everybody wants to talk about the past. It's a habit. People who try to help people think you need to talk about the past. You can if you want, but I discovered that you don't need to.

His book was published in 1960 and it was a revolution in psychology and self-image. Back then psychology had turned to pills, therapy, and analysis. It didn't seem logical to most people that taking control of your mind and thinking could *cure* you from your *dis*ease.

I WAS ON THE RIGHT TRACK ALL ALONG.

I'm not writing this to make you believe this or prove to you it works. I know what I know, and I've proved it time and time again to myself and others. If you need proof, then go ahead. You can spend your years studying and reading psychology, self-help books, and other works on the mind or brain like I did. Or you can take

---

1. Maxwell Maltz, *Psycho-Cybernetics Deluxe Edition: The Original Text of the Classic Guide to a New Life*, (New York: Tarcher-Perigee, 2016)

my word for it, and save yourself a lot of time, a lot of pain, and a lot of overthinking.

I was thinking about a young woman whom I had helped recently. She was struggling with her past trauma and was stuck "trying to figure out what was wrong" with her.

She had suffered abuse and trauma at the hands of family members and people she had trusted. When I met her, she had already spent years in different types of therapy, trying to figure out what was wrong and how to let go and move forward. She spent a lot of time digging into her past. I remember the call like it was yesterday.

I asked her some questions and got her perspective on her story and experiences and how she viewed her past. The combination of her trauma, the cultural beliefs she inherited, and her feeling of being different from her family caused her to doubt herself and take on way too much blame and shame. Then I asked her a simple question: "What if you could let all of this go simply and quickly?" I told her she could if she would be willing to change her perspective on what had happened to her.

I explained that the trauma and abuse was not about her. It simply happened to her and it didn't happen because of her and she shouldn't take it personally. That was the same cure for me. It took me a long time to reconcile that. It could've happened to anyone. In fact, it is happening to many, but it's not because of them. Too often victims carry the blame and the shame for their abuse. The system perpetuates a victim mentality. The cure to letting go is changing your perspective on what had happened. That's it! It's that simple. That's the cure.

These days the mental health system encourages us to talk about our story, over and over and over. I spent years in talk therapy, and it made me feel better . . . temporarily, for a few days or weeks, but it didn't change my perception of my story. I stayed stuck in my story. Dwelling on your past will not help your future.

> **The cure to letting go is changing your perspective on what had happened.**

You can let go of your past trauma. Change your perception on your mental health, and you'll discover there's nothing wrong with you. The only thing that is wrong is how you perceive yourself and what you've *been through*. There's nothing wrong when you don't feel right. It's human.

The cure lies within your own personal power to control what you think about you and what you believe to be true. Whatever you believe, must be true to you. Your subconscious is impersonal. It's completely deductive, and it accepts whatever you give it. The harsh reality is that you accept ideas and beliefs about your mental health and healing that may not be working, but you have the power to create new ideas and beliefs that can work for you.

■ MEDITATION ■

No, dear brothers and sisters, I have not achieved it,
but I focus on this one thing: Forgetting the past and
looking forward to what lies ahead, I press on to reach
the end of the race and receive the heavenly prize for
which God, through Christ Jesus, is calling us.

Philippians 3:13-14 NLT

■ INSIGHTS ■

What did you learn from this chapter?

1.

2.

3.

■ ACTION ■

As you can see, the cure to break free from the past is to make simple logical decisions. Most of what you're holding onto isn't logical anymore. You can argue this if you want, but you'll be defending a past that doesn't serve you.

- What are you dwelling on?
- If the cure is to let go of the past, and you'll feel better, then what do you need to let go of?

You bought this book because you're looking for direction to let go of a past that's holding you back. If you keep allowing your beliefs to fight me, you'll stay stuck. Do me a favor, if you won't listen, give this book to someone who will. What's it going to be?

CHAPTER 29

Who Do You Think You Are?

The people who are crazy enough to think they can change the world are the ones who do.

—Steve Jobs, co-founder of Apple

Stop thinking you don't deserve a good life, because you do.

Who do you think you are? Has anyone ever asked you that? Lots of people heard this from their parents, teachers, family members, or friends. Don't take it personally when people claim to see your limitations; it is only through their eyes. Their viewpoint got distorted when someone limited their view on themselves and that's why they say it to you. When someone asks you that, you can simply respond, "Who do you think I am, and why do you care? What you think about me is none of my business and it's none of yours. What you think of you is."

You may have a distorted self-worth. Your parents might have drilled that idea into your head. Did they ever say, "You don't deserve that"? Or perhaps you've been in situations or relationships where you were mistreated, and friends or family said, "You don't deserve that." Ironically, you think you *did* deserve it, and for some distorted reason you may think you still do now.

The problem is that people are seeking from other people the validation and confirmation that they're worthy. When they can't find it, they turn in the wrong direction, hoping the answer is there. People don't need advice on self-worth. That's only suggesting they aren't worthy.

> **If you have a dream of what you want to become *someday* you already are that person deep inside.**

Too many people are locked into the idea that they're not worthy. They are trying to get ahead in life and transform their story into something meaningful, but they're convinced, deep down, that they don't deserve the success they seek.

Unfortunately, we didn't have the awareness or self-confidence to stand up for our beliefs about ourselves. So, when we stake our claim and step out, we're shot down by people who have limiting beliefs from their own mistaken identity.

When people see limits in you, they see them in others, and to make themselves feel better about themselves, they criticize others. Most people who act like they are superior are really masking their own feelings of inferiority.

I believe most of the dreams we have for ourselves are not really dreams at all. If you have a dream of what you want to become *someday* you already are that person deep inside. If you have a desire to be something or do something, it means you have been gifted by God with the passion, talent, and abilities to carry it out. You are worthy of the task.

WHAT DO YOU REALLY WANT?

If you want to know who you are, just look at what you want. What are you passionate about? What do you really want? How do you truly want to live your life? If you knew you couldn't fail, what would you do? Whatever you want, you're worth it.

Whatever you want, you already are that person. Otherwise, you wouldn't want it. The problem is as soon as you connect to what you want, your mistaken identity kicks in and tells you that you don't deserve it, or it gives you a thousand and one excuses for why you can't do it. More lies!

Who do you think you are? That's a good question to ask yourself. If you're trying to find yourself in self-help books or therapy or asking others their opinions, you'll likely end up with the wrong answer.

If you ask the right person, you'll get the right answer. I don't mean you should go ask others. Even the ones who love you the most are not the ones to ask. There's only one place to go to find out who you are.

God placed desires in you and blessed you with gifts and talents. And God made no mistake in making you. If you want to find out who you think you are, ask Him what He thinks. Even if you don't believe in God, turn within and listen.

Most people are trying to convince themselves to become someone they're not. You can't become something or someone else just by willing it. You probably believe things about yourself that aren't true, even though you have hard evidence to prove that they are.

To adopt a new self-image, you must accept that the mistaken identity you've been living with is a lie. And there also must be some reason to believe that the new *you* is based on the truth.

Here's the truth, plain and simple: You think you're not worthy of the success you seek, but you are. At some point, you were convinced you're not, so you keep searching for the truth and doubting yourself. The truth is, you are a gift, and you have gifts. You are worth far more than you think. Whatever you desire in your heart, you deserve it. You're worth it, and you are that person already. How do I know this is true? Because this is resonating with you. It if wasn't true it wouldn't resonate with you so deeply. I know you can feel it!

That was hard for me to accept for a long time. When I started to entertain ideas of who I thought I was, what my gifts were, and how I might change the world, I got really scared. It's okay to be scared. You've been living with your false self for a long time, so when you meet your true self, it's a little uncomfortable.

> **You think you're not worthy of the success you seek, but you are.**

You don't need to create a new self-image. You already have that image inside you; otherwise you wouldn't want to be who you're hoping you can be. Your true self is covered up by your mistaken identity. I can't wait for you to meet your "true" self.

Perish the idea you need confirmation and validation. You don't. You're already worthy. Don't just take my word for it, take God's word for it. That beats therapy, self-help, and others' opinions hands down.

■ MEDITATION ■

For you created my inmost being; you knit me together in my mother's womb. I praise you because I am fearfully and wonderfully made; your works are wonderful, I know that full well.

Psalm 139:13–14 NIV

■ INSIGHTS ■

What did you learn from this chapter?

1.

2.

3.

▪ ACTION ▪

What do you want to do? Who do you want to become?

- If you knew you couldn't fail, no matter what, what would you do or become?
- Describe that person, and then realize this: that's who you already are.

When you think about what you really want for your life, you wouldn't want it unless you were that person, and you've been given all the talents and abilities to be that person.

CHAPTER 30

Check Out Your View

*Life is really simple, but we insist
on making it complicated.*

—Confucius

WHEN YOU READ THE QUOTE ABOVE, I IMAGINE WHAT
YOU MIGHT BE THINKING. LIFE *IS* HARD; *I* DON'T MAKE
IT HARD.

This is the final chapter in this book, but it could
be the beginning of a new and better life for you or
anyone who reads this.

There are two words I want you to remember. I
suggest you make them your lens through which you
view the world and what happens to you. They are *perception* and *judgment*.

The way you view people, situations, and circumstances in your life passes through the lens of your own judgment. If your life seems hard, it's because you have judged it to be hard. That's a decision you made.

Life is challenging but it isn't hard! Look around you at all the things you have, what you're able to do, and the freedoms you enjoy. If your judgment of your situation causes you to perceive it as hard, then that's up to you to change your mind. Life isn't hard, but how you're thinking about it is hard.

> **If your life seems hard, it's because you have judged it to be hard.**

Just because your brain is processing information, that doesn't mean you're thinking. What are you thinking? That's a good question! Stop right here for a moment and think about what you think about. Become an observer and pay attention to how you perceive and judge your world and the world you live in. Do you react to the world or are you in control of your thinking?

Until you train your mind and take control of your inner world (your thinking), life will be hard. Your inner world controls how you perceive and judge your outer world and how you react to it.

If you feel you're a victim to your outer world, perish the thought. A victim mentality will not serve you. Nobody wants to be around a victim, and the people who want to support victims often perpetuate the victim's own victim mentality.

Let me explain.

Shortly after my story came out, a woman contacted me through the newspaper article. Her son had been sexually abused by one of the same men who abused me. The man was facing more charges in court. He was convicted as a "dangerous offender." The mom asked if I would meet with her son and talk to him. Of course, I agreed.

I remember walking up his driveway and seeing this skinny young boy approach me. His head hung low, he couldn't make eye contact, and when I shook his hand, his palm was sweaty. He was me twenty-six years earlier. We spoke for a while, and he shared his story. He wanted to speak up and tell his story like I had, but he was fourteen and, by law, his identity was being kept hidden to protect him. He had gone to the newspapers to speak up but they couldn't publish his story.

I think that was a mistake. I think the law doesn't always protect children; I think it fosters their shame and contributes to their feeling like a victim because the system treats them like a victim. Most people feel like victims because they think they are victims. That judgment about themselves prevents them from recovering sooner. Not everyone recovers from the trauma of abuse, but some do! Anyone can; not everyone will.

Sometimes people think there's something special about me. What's really special about my recovery and triumph is the people along the way who convinced me that I wasn't a victim and that I could take control of my thinking.

I see my past as a gift. The abuse and trauma and all the mistakes I've made as a symptom of the abuse are all gifts. Mistakes are like that. They are lessons that can be gifts if you see them that way.

I hope you let go of the past that's holding you back.

I like my view now! Life isn't hard; life is good.

Does it get hard sometimes? Yes! But I remember two simple words: *perception* and *judgment*.

I hope you take control of your thinking and your life. I hope you let go of the past that's holding you back. I hope that you step up and help others to free themselves from their mistaken identity. If you're reading this book, you've been given a good start. Now the rest is up to you.

My wish for you is that you'll let go of your mistaken identity and free yourself from your emotional prison. Let go of the past that's holding you back. You won't find your purpose in your past. It's waiting for you in your future. When you drop your mistaken identity, you'll clear your name, and you'll meet your true self.

■ MEDITATION ■

And we know that God causes everything to work together for the good of those who love God and are called according to his purpose for them.

Romans 8:28 NLT

■ INSIGHTS ■

What did you learn from this chapter?

1.

2.

3.

■ ACTION ■

Your last action step is the only one you'll need going forward.

- ■ Create a single affirmation that tells you the truth of who you are. Then repeat it often until you believe the truth, and the truth makes you free.

Here's mine if you want to borrow it: *I am a good person. I am a gift to the world, and I have been given gifts that I will use to help change the world. I am in control of my thinking and my life.*

Amen!

POSTLUDE
The Bottom Line

THIS BOOK WAS written for you and for people like you and me. The stories and experiences I shared were shared openly and transparently in the hope that they will inspire you to let go of a past that's holding you back. You can stop living in an emotional prison, and you can break out. You're stuck because it's a case of mistaken identity. Discover your true self and be yourself, and you'll be set free.

Transformation comes by changing your mind. Healing comes from letting go. Being yourself comes by ridding yourself of judgment and criticism. Guilt falls away when you stop living in the past, and shame releases its grip on you when you forgive yourself for your mistakes and your past.

This book is meant to be simple. Healing is simple. Letting go of the past is simple.

HERE'S THE BOTTOM LINE.

There are three things you need to do to let go of a past that's holding you back.

1. Learn how your mind works, and take control of what you think about.
2. Stop looking back on the past with guilt and resentment, and stop worrying about your future and creating anxiety.
3. Drop your "poor me," victim mindset by letting go of your suffering.

This can be simple; it can happen fast, and it doesn't need to be complicated. Many won't accept that idea, and that's why it's hard. Throughout this book, I gave you simple instructions to follow each day, which will lead to your transformation. If it worked for me, it can work for you.

Remember this piece of Scripture: "Do not conform to the pattern of this world, but be transformed by the renewing of your mind" (Romans 12:2 NIV).

My hope is you will *let* the principles and exercises work *on* you. Don't force them. Renew your mind by changing your mind, and let God, nature, and the universe take care of the rest.

Most of your struggles are internal. In other words, it's how you're looking at your past, your current situation, and your future that causes your suffering. Now don't get me wrong, I'm not minimizing your situation. I don't know you or what you've been through.

What I know is this: if you change your mind and your perception of your past, present, and future, you will be calmer and more confident to solve your problems objectively so your problems don't control you.

Guilt falls away when you stop living in the past.

Only you can control your thinking and take charge of your life. Nobody is going to do it for you, but you *can* do it. You can break free of the past and your mistaken identity, and you will find your purpose.

Don't forget, you were created in God's image, and you were designed for a purpose, not for suffering. But your suffering can be converted into good if you choose to let it.

ACKNOWLEDGMENTS

I HAVE A HEART filled with gratitude for my mentor and friend Bob Proctor who was patient and kind as he waited for me to accept how simple it was to let go of my past.

Elena, you got me to believe I was ready for this book, and it was time to share it. And you helped me chisel away at the raw material and keep uncovering the hidden gems. You are a gift!

Jay, you introduced me to God and suggested I partner with Him and partner up what I had learned about mindset with what He would teach me.

Thank you to my friend Pete for bringing helpful scriptures to the book that could help others.

To everyone else that believed in me when I didn't, you nudged me and encouraged me and for that I'm grateful.